— THE —

WAIT

—— THE ——
WAIT

A POWERFUL PRACTICE TO
FINDING THE LOVE OF YOUR LIFE

AND THE LIFE YOU LOVE

DEVON FRANKLIN
AND MEAGAN GOOD

WITH TIM VANDEHEY

HOWARD BOOKS

NEW YORK   LONDON   TORONTO   SYDNEY   NEW DELHI

HOWARD BOOKS

An Imprint of Simon & Schuster, Inc.
1230 Avenue of the Americas
New York, NY 10020

Scripture quotations marked (NLT) are taken from the Holy Bible, New Living Translation, copyright © 1996, 2004, 2007. Used by permission of Tyndale House Publishers Inc., Carol Stream, Illinois 60188. All rights reserved.

Scripture quotations marked (NIV) are taken from THE HOLY BIBLE, NEW INTERNATIONAL VERSION®, NIV® Copyright © 1973, 1978, 1984, 2011 by Biblica, Inc.® Used by Permission of Biblica, Inc.® All rights reserved worldwide.

Scripture quotations marked (MSG) are taken from The Message. Copyright © 1993, 1994, 1995, 1996, 2000, 2001, 2002. Used by permission of NavPress Publishing Group.

First Howard Books trade paperback edition March 2017

HOWARD and colophon are trademarks of Simon & Schuster, Inc.

For information about special discounts for bulk purchases, please contact Simon & Schuster Special Sales at 1-866-506-1949 or business@simonandschuster.com.

The Simon & Schuster Speakers Bureau can bring authors to your live event. For more information or to book an event, contact the Simon & Schuster Speakers Bureau at 1-866-248-3049 or visit our website at www.simonspeakers.com.

Manufactured in the United States of America

10   9

Library of Congress Cataloging-in-Publication Data is available.

ISBN 978-1-5011-0529-6
ISBN 978-1-5011-2348-1 (pbk)
ISBN 978-1-5011-0531-9 (ebook)

This book is dedicated to everyone who believes love is a "gift." To those who are willing to choose an ultimate journey of self-discovery and allow this gift to come into their lives at God's appointed time, in its purest form. We know firsthand how scary this can be, but if you are willing to trust God, have courage, and wait for that kind of love you deserve, it will enhance every area of their life.

Contents

Introduction

It was the first time we held hands, and we'll never forget it. It wasn't romantic. We weren't gazing longingly into each other's eyes. We just grabbed each other as we shouldered through a Hollywood mob that blocked our way like the Red Sea. But it was a moment that we'll both remember for the rest of our lives.

It was the spring of 2011 in Los Angeles, and it was our second date. Sort of. On our first date, at the Stone Rose Lounge at the Sofitel, we talked for hours about life, family, career, goals, and the Lord. It was nice, but when it was over it felt . . . platonic. We had known each other professionally for four years at that point, and although we felt attracted to each other, we weren't sure that there was really anything going on. Then came the Prince concert at the House of Blues on the Sunset Strip. The place was so thick with fans, celebrities, media, and security that there was barely any room to breathe. We decided to make a mad dash through the throng to reach some people we knew, clasped hands so we wouldn't get separated . . . and it hit us.

A physical-spiritual concussion, like a jolt of electricity to the heart. It was like something from a rom-com script so cliché-ridden that it gets sent to turnaround (the film industry term for a project that a film studio decides not to develop further). Our eyes met, and it was clear that we had both felt it. It was as though two souls that God had been guiding toward each other for years had navigated all the plot twists and jumped all the obstacles to come together at last. In fact, that's exactly what happened.

After the concert, we stood outside and talked, oblivious to everyone and everything else.

MEAGAN: Some people had labeled me a wild party girl because of what they read on blogs or in the tabloids. But that night, DeVon told me that wasn't the person he saw. He said he could see my heart. I was in tears. I felt like somebody other than my family was finally seeing *me,* not the person people were quick to judge me to be. Then he said, "God doesn't show your heart to everybody. He only shows it to people He can trust with it."

DEVON: That wasn't planned; it was straight from the heart. It was like God had spoken those words to my spirit and they just flowed out of me. I remember over the years seeing Meagan in the media, and there was always something about her that I knew was more than meets the eye.

But even though the sparks were flying, we didn't kiss. The timing wasn't right. Why force it?

On our third date, we caught a movie at the Sherman Oaks Galleria. Afterward, we ended up sitting in Meagan's car for an hour and a half talking about how young people needed positive influences from Hollywood. We watched funny YouTube videos and looked at old pictures. Then we got out of the car and talked for another hour, standing in the partially vacated parking lot. Then we hugged for what felt like an eternity. Finally, as we said good night for what must have been the tenth time, we had our first kiss. As our lips touched, we could feel the Spirit of God surround and embrace us. Instantly, we were both euphoric in the Spirit, miles high. It was like a confirmation that this was right.

You can talk about God being in your life, but there is nothing like actually feeling God's hand moving in your life. This was God moving in our lives, and it was incredible.

WHY WE WAITED

However, even with all that electricity flying, we were cautious. We didn't lose our heads. We didn't dash off to Las Vegas for a ten-minute ceremony at a drive-through chapel. It wasn't just about gushing to friends and family members that we'd finally found "the One." And as millions of people know from our many post-wedding magazine interviews, radio and television appearances, and live talks, we waited until after we got married to have sex.

When we began talking publicly about our courtship and our celibacy, the questions from hosts and audience members naturally started off being mostly about sex. Giggling like teenagers in a locker room, people would ask the obvious: How did we stay strong? How did we resist temptation? Things like that. Both of us answered honestly and clearly from our experiences, and in time the questioning became deeper and more serious. There was a desire, a hunger, behind the inquiries. The unspoken message was: *We want to have real love. Is it really possible? Your love appears to be so real. If it is, tell us how you got it, please.*

So we started looking at the choices that had taken us from being two coworkers in the entertainment business to being a blissfully happy husband and wife, sitting in front of audiences talking about how we'd made it work. As we did, a pattern revealed itself. Again and again, faced with the choice between instant gratification and delaying our own satisfaction to pursue something better, we chose the latter. When we weren't even together but were coming out of unhappy relationships, we each chose not to be intimate (intimacy isn't just about sex; it's also about sharing emotionally) with anyone for a time. When we grew closer but were unsure whether we were really right for each other, we waited for clarity from God. When we felt those incredible second- and third-date connections, we didn't go crazy, get engaged, or even jump into a relationship the next day. We waited and got to know each other. As our physical attraction grew stronger, we resolved to wait until after marriage. Faced with choice after choice, when it would have been easy and fun to throw caution and good sense to the wind, we waited.

But why? Why did we consciously delay the gratification—not just sexual but emotional and spiritual—that would have come with diving headfirst into a passionate relationship? The answer is simple: we wanted God's very best for our lives, collectively and individually, and we wanted it in whatever way He intended. This required patience.

In the past, we'd both been burned in unpleasant relationships because we acted impulsively, leaped before we looked, or let our emotions overwhelm our judgment. We got tired of doing things the same way but expecting a different result (this is the classic definition of insanity). Maybe there was a way God wanted us to date that would bring us peace and what we wanted most: *authentic love*.

The signs that He was guiding us toward each other were unmistakable, but He didn't want us to come together before we were ready. So we were still. We examined who we were, what we needed, and the mistakes we'd made in past relationships. We began the process of letting go of some heavy baggage and some preconceptions about the kind of person who might make a perfect partner. In short, we quit trying to make things happen for our short-term pleasure and let God take the wheel.

When we finally got together and talked about the experiences leading up to our relationship, we understood that we had discovered something profound and powerful. By consciously not giving in to the desire for a quick hit of satisfaction—the intoxicating rush of a new romance, the flush of sexual attraction, the pleasure of having someone to show off to friends and family—we laid the groundwork for what has become the love of our lives.

Because we waited, we exchanged immediate gratification for what we really wanted and who we really wanted to be. Because we waited, God was able to reveal things that we would have missed if we had been blinded by the white-hot light of lust, desperate to fulfill our own desires. Because we waited, we were eventually ready.

That was the beginning of The Wait.

YES, THE WAIT IS (SORT OF) ABOUT SEX

The Wait is not just about sex, but it begins with sex. How could it not? We live in a time when books like the *Fifty Shades of Grey* trilogy have sold more than 100 million copies and the corresponding movie has grossed over half a billion dollars at the worldwide box office. Almost every popular magazine on the newsstands has some headline dealing with sex. "I Like High-End Sex Parties and I'm Not a Weirdo" was an actual headline from one of the biggest magazines in the world. Well, how about "We Waited to Have Sex and We're Not Weirdos Either"?

Human beings love sex. We think about it, talk about it, read about it, watch it on the Internet, and spend a great deal of our time, energy, and money trying to get it. Because of this, sex makes us do some truly stupid things. Ironically, as much as we like to wag our fingers at one another about the potential harm our hypersexual culture can cause, talking about *not* having sex is what raises people's ire. The moment the two of us announced we were working on this book, a prominent blog published a post titled "Meagan Good, DeVon Franklin & the Danger of Promoting 'The Wait.'" We had no idea that talking about our story and trying to provide a positive, healthy dialogue about relationships and sex would be deemed dangerous!

We actually think it's dangerous *not* to talk about sex

and advocate the idea that it's okay to wait. How can you learn to date in a way that promotes physical, spiritual, and mental health if you don't talk about the emotional, spiritual, and physical risks of sex? Is it really okay for the majority of songs on the radio—and the melodies streaming through Spotify and thousands of HD music videos on Vevo—to market an oversexualized way of life to the masses but not okay for us to talk about an alternative way of thinking that might actually help someone become a healthier person and lead a better life?

We're also not the only ones talking about this. Russell Wilson, Super Bowl–winning Seattle Seahawks quarterback and an outspoken Christian, shocked fans when, during a Q&A at a church in San Diego last summer, he announced that he and his girlfriend, singer and dancer Ciara Harris, had decided to abstain from sex—or as Russell described it, doing it "Jesus's way." The media went crazy. As news website *The Root* put it in a headline, "Russell Wilson and Ciara Aren't Having Sex and It's Everybody's Business." Like it or not, waiting for sex is in the conversation and a lot more people are recognizing that it's an idea that's at least worth talking about.

But does it matter what the two of us—or Russell and Ciara—say? From a spiritual standpoint, what does the Bible say on this matter? Here are two key scriptures we find to be extremely compelling:

God's will is for you to be holy, so stay away from all sexual sin.
(1 THESSALONIANS 4:3, NLT)

You know the old saying, "First you eat to live, and then you live to eat"? Well, it may be true that the body is only a temporary thing, but that's no excuse for stuffing your body with food, or indulging it with sex. Since the Master honors you with a body, honor him with your body!

God honored the Master's body by raising it from the grave. He'll treat yours with the same kind of power. Until that time, remember that your body was created with the same dignity as the Master's body. You wouldn't take the Master's body off to a whorehouse, would you? I should hope not.

There's more to sex than mere skin on skin. Sex is as much spiritual mystery as physical fact. As written in Scripture, "The two become one." Since we want to become spiritually one with the Master, we must not pursue the kind of sex that avoids commitment and intimacy, leaving us more lonely than ever— the kind of sex that can never help us become one. Sexual sins are different from all others. In sexual sin we violate the sacredness of our own bodies, these bodies that were made for God-given and God-modeled love—for "becoming one" with another. Or didn't you realize that your body is a sacred place, the place of the Holy Spirit? Don't you see that you can't live however you please, squandering what God paid such a high

price for? The physical part of you is not some piece of prop-
erty belonging to the spiritual part of you. God owns the whole
works. So let people see God in and through your body.

(1 CORINTHIANS 6:13–20, MSG)

However, despite what Scripture says, people (Christian or not) are going to have sex. We find our reasons and justifications. The faith-minded might rationalize that waiting doesn't apply if you're dating the one you believe you're going to marry. Physically, we need and want sex, and it's just hard to resist those hormones. Socially, even the mention of going without sex is met with snickers and stares.

There's nothing wrong with sex or sexuality. God created both for the enjoyment of married couples. But for too long, there's been an ugly stigma associated with sex, the church, and where it all fits in the reality of the world we live in. Our hope is that we can finally open up a healthy dialogue that resonates with you and everyone who reads it. We would like this book to become a positive cultural conversation starter as we all strive to live our God-given destiny with emotional, spiritual, and physical health. We're not sex experts and this isn't a book about religious reasons not to have sex. It's our story, and we want to share what has worked for us.

When we took sex off the table, our minds were clearer, our access to God was crisper, and we were able to make better decisions in other important areas of our relationship that weren't related to sex at all. Once we did that, we saw that applying The Wait to other aspects of relationships could really be beneficial, too. The Wait is about getting control of your life, reducing the dating drama, and avoiding desperate relationship choices so that you can make better decisions about your future.

ANSWERS TO THE IMPORTANT QUESTIONS

We know many people who have struggled with finding not only lasting happiness in their relationships but also peace within themselves. The two are of a piece: until you know and love yourself, it's hard to find anyone else to love you the way you deserve. The practice of waiting—choosing to wait for sex and denying instant gratification so that you can see clearly, make better decisions, and position yourself for blessings—is the key to finding not just happiness but spirit-deep fulfillment.

We live in a culture addicted to the quick hookup, the miracle cure, and the overnight sensation. The Wait is the remedy for that addiction.

With all its ups and downs, our love story is a bit like a rom-com movie of its own. We're going to share them with you: first meetings, shocking surprises, tantalizing signs, embarrassing twists, and a stirring resolution. To know that God had us in mind for each other all along and was waiting patiently for us to listen to him is thrilling and humbling at the same time.

The process of waiting was the key to our storybook beginning. The Wait isn't just a matter of stopping, sitting on the couch, and saying, "Okay, Lord, bless me." There's a lot more to it. Waiting has nothing to do with lying back and hoping that good things find you. It's about putting aside distractions, using your gifts, and becoming someone God can trust to bless with great opportunities and wonderful people.

Discovering this powerful process has brought us the kind of authentic, deep joy that comes with knowing we are truly meant to be together in every way—that we see and appreciate each other for the fullness of who we are, flaws and all. That's something we simply could not keep to ourselves. We hope we can give you a bit of insight into how God is working in your own life and help you ask the really important questions:

- Why haven't I found true love yet?
- How are some of my habits working *against* the life I really want?

- What have I been spending my energy and attention on and why?
- What have I been compromising to do that?
- What am I ready to sacrifice to become my best self?
- Do I need help making healthier choices for my life?

In *The Wait,* we hope to give you the answers to those questions. We'll offer specific advice for men and women and tell you what we've learned about the power of being still, working to become the best version of yourself, and allowing God to bring His vision of your life to fruition. In the end, we hope you'll be entertained, moved, and most important, inspired to try this powerful tool for yourself. We think you'll see that there's nothing boring, passive, or docile about waiting. Done right, it's actually the most potent force imaginable for creating the life you crave . . . the life God wants you to have.

God bless you now and always,
DeVon and Meagan

CHAPTER ONE

NO SEX? YOU CAN'T BE SERIOUS

Patience is not the ability to Wait,
but the ability to keep a good attitude while Waiting.
— JOYCE MEYERS

Just what is The Wait, exactly? The Wait is a conscious choice to pursue delayed gratification in the areas of life specifically related to relationships. It's a decision to get your mind right, figure out who you want to be and what you want out of life, and use your time and energy to become the best version of yourself. Put simply:

To Wait is to delay the temptation for instant gratification
in relationships in order to get what you really want in life
and become the person you truly want to be.

That starts with saying no to sex. The Wait isn't 100

percent about sex, but that's where it begins. Sex is probably the most compelling aspect of human gratification. It's such a powerful desire that outside of a proper healthy context it can cloud our judgment and cause us to make decisions that work against our own best self-interest. The untamed, untempered drive for sexual gratification has toppled empires, scuttled political careers, destroyed marriages, and squandered fortunes. Sex can be like a McLaren F1 race car: great in the right hands, but potentially disastrous when handled recklessly.

We're willing to bet that you've experienced more of the latter. We know because we've done it. We've all made terrible decisions about who to flirt with, spend time with, commit to, and even sleep with that had nothing to do with our brains but everything to do with our bodies. Sex can become a gateway drug to all kinds of other choices intended to satisfy the need for quick pleasure: going out with that gorgeous girl even though you know she's a hot mess, spending the weekend at that dude's place even though you know you're not the only one, or having just one more drink even though you know it will impair your judgment.

When we chase the high of instant gratification, we make choices that for many reasons are irresponsible and based on poor reasoning . . . or no reasoning at all. It takes time and self-control to take in information, let people reveal their true character, be consistent and disciplined, and give conflicts time to work themselves out. Delaying gratification means working at becoming more self-aware and humble enough to admit that our first impulses aren't always smart ones.

Let's be really, really clear on this:

One of the keys to practicing The Wait is giving up sex.

We know that for many Christians and non-Christians alike, the idea of giving up sex is too outrageous and impossible to consider. We get that. Yet based on our experience, we still believe that practicing The Wait until marriage will set you up for success and align you with God's perfect will for your life in all areas.

SEX, WAITING, AND RELATIONSHIPS

At its heart *The Wait* is a book about relationships, but there's no unwinding the connection between relationships and sexuality. Love and sex are the two sides of the same coin. When you have sex with someone outside of marriage, you're not just setting off a chain of chemical reactions in your brain that make you think they're a lot better for you than they probably are; you're giving them a part of your spirit.

When you have sex with someone, you really are leaving them a piece of yourself and taking a part of them with you . . . whether you want to or not. So each sex partner, good and bad, becomes a part of your future. Does this make you think twice about who you choose—and have chosen—to get into bed with?

Sex is an act of trust. It's about way more than physical attraction—yet when you think of it only as physical attraction you will see (or have already seen) that attraction lies and spellbinds. Strong relationships aren't built solely on physical or sexual attraction. They're built on good judgment. How many times have you become caught up with someone based mostly on sexual attraction? How have those relationships ended?

We don't have to ask *if* they've ended, because they don't last. They can't. Before too long, the hormonal haze clears and all that matters is character, integrity, intelligence, values, spirituality, and self-esteem. A person who doesn't have enough of those to suit you is a person you can't tolerate for long.

Delaying gratification and getting greater control over your behavior—so that you can break the patterns that keep sabotaging you—is the key to finally finding the life and the peace that you hunger for. It's the key to becoming who you've always aspired to be, an idea we'll unpack in chapter two. But it all starts with giving up sex.

THE PROBLEM WITH SEX

Sex, of course, is a topic overflowing with religious, cultural, political, and personal baggage. Much of our popular culture is built around sexual titillation. In our business, the making of movies and television, actors are often cast as much for their good looks as for their acting talents. You don't really think that all private detectives look like Denzel Washington, do you?

As a people, we're alternately conflicted, fascinated, and appalled by sex in all its forms. Lawmakers crusade against pornography while their constituents consume it in record amounts. Abstinence-only sex-education programs deny teens basic information on the assumption that it will make them promiscuous, while the data show that teens are less sexually active than they've been in decades. The most popular magazines seem to be about nothing *but* sex: how to get it, how to give it, where to have it, how to be better at it, how to know if your partner is having it with someone else, and so on. We're obsessed with sex, and at the same time we disapprove of our obsession. It's no wonder that sex ties us in knots.

An old saying goes, "Success makes us forgetful and stupid." Sex does the same thing. It makes us forget who we are and what we want. It makes us do things that we look at later and say, "What was I thinking?"

After we got married in 2012, we were asked to appear at numerous conferences and gatherings all around the country to share the story of our relationship and how God brought us together. Though we talked about personal growth and getting closer to God, the stories about us—online and off-line—mostly focused on one thing: waiting to have sex. No matter how deep our faith and how intense our devotion and duty to God, we're still human, and human beings tend to be like twelve-year-olds when it comes to the topic of sex. (LOL).

Sex is pleasurable. Sex between two people who love each other body and soul is transcendent. But more often than not, that's not the kind of sex most people are having. A good friend of ours once said to us, "I'm not getting married until I have what you guys have." That's flattering and humbling, but it's also a reflection on how hard it is to find compatibility.

The two of us are not anti-sex. To be anti-sex would pretty much be the same as being anti-God. God created sex and we fully advocate the joy of experiencing it the way He intended. What we do know is that we've seen and known a lot of people whose higher aspirations for love, family, and success have landed on the rocks because they put the pursuit of sex before anything else.

The question, "to have sex or not to have sex?" is at the heart of The Wait. That's not because the most popular question when we spoke at Morehouse College or at T. D. Jakes's MegaFest or on *Jimmy Kimmel Live!* was "How did you manage not to have sex?" It's because we saw the incredible and undeniable grace that came to our relationship when we decided to remain committed to celibacy before marriage.

WHY WE CHOSE TO BE CELIBATE

We both discovered independently that to be the people we truly wanted to be, we needed to take sex out of the equation.

DEVON: I had made a commitment of celibacy long before I met Meagan. When we got married, I had been celibate for over ten years. What motivated the commitment was the same thing that made me keep it. I was preaching about living a life that put the Lord first, and then I was going out and living a life that was the opposite of the discipline I was teaching. Trying to be two people started tearing me apart. The desire for peace and harmony within myself was a motivator to choose no sex.

I asked myself, "What if what I was doing with this other woman disqualified me for the full manifestation of the call that God has on my life? Would it be worth it?" Of course not! No sex is worth that! I could not reconcile the idea that at the end of my life God might say, "Here's what I had planned for you, but because you showed yourself unworthy, I couldn't do all I wanted to do in your life." I was not prepared to take that risk. Whatever my purpose is in this life, I didn't want anything to get in the way of that.

MEAGAN: I got saved when I was twelve and lost my virginity when I was nineteen. As a Christian, I felt a strong conviction about not having sex, but like most of us, I made excuses and swept those convictions under the rug. And in some relationships I tried hard to abstain; in others I just guiltily went with the flow because I had failed miserably, so what was the point. On some occasions I opted to not even acknowledge my reservations at all because the guilt was exhausting. I repeated the same painful patterns in my relationships over and over, but I didn't connect that to sex for a long time.

Finally, I knew I had to make a commitment to take sex off the table. I knew I couldn't do the same thing and expect a different result. I knew I was giving most of me but not all of me at this point. I already knew DeVon but didn't know he was my husband. By the time I began to entertain the thought of celibacy, my life was an emotional mess. Going celibate helped me clean it up in all areas (even areas where sex played no part). If I hadn't done that, I doubt we would have come together as husband and wife.

Later, when we got together and got the memo—the revelation that our relationship was going to happen and in fact was meant to be—we didn't want to do anything to sabotage it. Since we had both been celibate at this point, we agreed that we would remain celibate until after we married . . . if we married. So we took a calculated risk: we would forego physical pleasure so that we could really get to know each other's minds, hearts, and spirits and confirm that God was truly bringing us together.

Considering the potential payoff, it wasn't much of a risk. Sure, we were passing up sexual gratification. But by achieving real clarity we avoided making a life-altering mistake either way. Of course, things did work out. We fell in love with each other as whole people, and the promised payoff has been a life filled with not just joy but the peace that comes with knowing we're firmly in the center of God's purpose.

Now, we won't lie to you. It wasn't always easy. There were nights when things would get hot and heavy and Meagan would stop us and say, "I can't get down like this. I'm used to going all the way. So we need to cool off." And we would stop right there, say our good nights, and part for the evening. That happened plenty of times.

But when it dawned on us just how important celibacy was for our union, we both said, "Lord, delaying gratification is powerful!"

How powerful? We saw the many ways that God blessed us and continues to bless us with a relationship built on mutual respect and deep understanding of who we are. We didn't let sex distort our perceptions, cloud our judgment, or make us rationalize something we didn't like. We fell in love as centered, intelligent people and children of God long before we fell in love with each other's physicality or sensuality.

WHAT THE WAIT *ISN'T*

Despite all this, The Wait is anything but passive. You're not sitting on your hands and hoping that things will turn out all right. You're making deliberate, positive choices that change who you are and how your mind works. You're also taking the resources you've been spending to chase after sexual gratification and using them instead to improve yourself in body, mind, and spirit.

We call this "strategic patience." While you wait, you're not putting your life on hold or wasting time waiting for something to happen. Instead, you're taking all the time and attention that you've been projecting outward and turning it inward. That's one of the most positive, life-affirming choices a person can make. From this perspective, you can finally see that hurling yourself into the path of potentially romantic relationships hasn't brought you any closer to what you want. It's time to try a different approach: letting love and purpose manifest in your life as a result of you working on becoming the best version of yourself.

Practicing strategic patience means understanding the difference between the two types of waiting:

1. Waiting that you choose.
2. Waiting that you have no choice about.

There's a big difference between something you choose and something that's forced upon you. With the first, you're in control; with the second, you resent control being taken from you. The Wait is about changing your circumstance from the second type of waiting into the first. Instead of feeling resentful and angry when the pursuit of your desires hits a wall, think, "Okay, since I'm already waiting, I'm going to choose to use this time productively." Your circumstances haven't changed, but how you see them certainly has. Just like that you transform yourself from passive victim into active collaborator with God.

Other things The Wait is not:

- *A punishment.* God isn't making you spend time alone as payback for some previous sin.
- *Forever.* We understand that not having sex is hard and could make a month feel like a year. But tell us this: What's the longest time in recent years that you've gone without sex against your will—Days? Weeks? Months? Years? Could you do that again, this time because you choose to?
- *Putting your life on hold.* Hardly. Now you have time and bandwidth to work on *you.* There are definitely times when fast, aggressive action is required to get what you want. You can still practice The Wait while you're actively going after all God has for you in life.
- *Weird.* We want to take the stigma away from waiting. What's bizarre about valuing yourself, your body, and your God over all else? Especially if you've already

been through the pain of multiple bad breakups, there's nothing weird about waiting, no matter what anyone else says.

Most important, The Wait isn't powerless. Though you might not see it, God has His hand on your life during this time, rearranging the scenery in order to set you up for good things to come.

THINGS TO KNOW ABOUT BEING CELIBATE

If only those facts were enough to convince people about the power of celibacy, but they're not. When we talk about The Wait and suggest that people consider going without sex, we get stares of horror. Many people can't even fathom going without sex for three months, much less years. On the male side, a lot of men have bought into the false idea that says that being a man means chasing lots of women. In that scenario, a man's worth has nothing to do with his character, morals, or integrity. It becomes reduced to how many women he sleeps with.

As for women, our culture tells them that their sexuality is one of the most important things they have to offer and then shames them for displaying it. It's really not surprising that sex provokes insecurity and internal conflicts. The unchecked premarital pursuit of sex can debase and objectify us, drive us further away from God's plan for our life, and expose us to incurable STDs, unplanned pregnancies, and tons of emotional trauma. So why is it that more of us don't just stop?

Well, we like sex. We crave it. Our bodies are designed to want sex in the way an addict wants drugs. Faced with celibacy, we rationalize. We say, "I don't know how to be celibate." Or, "We weren't meant to abstain." The problem is that *what we should do is not what we want to do*. It's a perfect example of instant gratification at war with delayed gratification.

Are you staying in a relationship for the sex and telling yourself that the other person will change one of these days? Well, has he or she changed yet? Maybe you've wrecked relationships and friendships by sleeping with multiple partners, even after swearing that you wouldn't. Maybe you're tired of the empty feeling you get when you wake up next to someone you slept with because you were lonely or had too much to drink. Perhaps it feels like you're on a treadmill of discouraging, drama-filled relationships based on physical attraction and not much else.

Any of that sound familiar? Then, we think that you know exactly what to do. You may even be getting some pretty clear signals from God about trying celibacy, but you don't want to go there. You don't want the questions, the pressure from friends, and the rejection of potential partners uninterested in waiting for sex. You think you'll be shunned or treated like some sort of freak. But there's probably a lot you don't know about celibacy:

More people are practicing it than you might think. According to studies by the Centers for Disease Control and Prevention and the National Institutes of Health, about 3 percent of Americans currently remain celibate until their honeymoons. That might not seem like a lot, but that means that about 5 million couples married today fell in love, vowed to wait, and kept that commitment intact until after they were joined in holy matrimony. So it can be done.

Celibacy is about the mind as much as it is about the body. When we think about celibacy, we focus on the physical need to have sex. But being celibate isn't just about pushing down that hormonal need to engage in intercourse. It's about owning how you feel, even when those horny feelings are coming on. It's choosing to discipline the mind and think of the benefit you seek, something that is greater than the desire to give in.

You might have heard people say something like this when talking about weight loss: "You have to think like a healthy person." It means that losing weight isn't entirely about changing what you eat, but about understanding why you eat the way you do. If you overeat out of anxiety or lone-liness and you can address those problems, you will change how you think about food and eat differently. Celibacy is the same. If you look at the reasons sex is important to you, you'll probably find that they are less important than having what you want in life and getting closer to God. That will change how you think about sex and make it easier to resist your physical urges.

The urges will still be there, make no mistake. They were there for us while we dated. We were tempted all the time. But our purpose was more important. Many of us don't even consider that the sexual aspect of a relationship *could be op-tional*. It doesn't occur to us. But what if it did? What if we made the conscious choice to make clarity and communica-tion and closeness more important than sexual gratification?

That's what the two of us mean by celibacy being about the mind. Once you reframe sex as a choice, you can reframe celibacy as a commitment that will help you get the things you want. Your sexual urges lose their power over you. You gain power over them.

DEVON: When I made the commitment to celibacy, I got a lot of disbelieving comments from friends. You should have seen the open mouths when I told people that I had remained celibate for more than ten years before marrying Meagan! But my friends' shock passed, and some of them said that they admired what I was doing. They knew I loved the Lord and that I was making this commitment out of a desire to be closer to him. In the end, some of them even said I inspired them to try it themselves.

As a man, if you can be disciplined in your sexual life, there's nothing you can't do. The discipline that you create in that area of your life will be the same for the rest of your life. The Bible says, "Give your gifts in private, and your Father, who sees everything, will reward you" (Matthew 6:4, NLT).

Celibacy isn't about shame or moral judgment. We'll say it again: we are not anti-sex. But some people are. They fear sex because it's a powerful motivator of behavior, and they judge those who have sex out of wedlock as morally inferior. Do not listen to those people when you're deciding whether or not to be celibate. Shame and the fear of being judged are the wrong reasons to practice The Wait. If you let yourself be shamed into it, you won't stick with it.

Sex isn't sinful. Sometimes people of faith have strange, outdated ideas about what sex is. Once again: sex itself is not sinful. Sex isn't wrong. God created the sexual act and the physical and emotional drives that make us want to have sex.

Sex is an act of creation, even if it doesn't result in a child. It creates joy and intimacy between two people. God-ordained sex between two people who are committed to each other in marriage, who know each other fully and are giving of themselves to each other, body and spirit—that is sanctified.

SIGNS FROM GOD

God won't leave you guessing. He will send you signs that it's time to slow down, quiet your mind, and work on yourself while He labors on your behalf. But it's up to you to read the signs that it's time to wait. They include:

- A breakup
- Physical or mental or emotional exhaustion
- Negative or hurtful people leaving your life
- The feeling of being lost or purposeless
- An opportunity to go on a long trip or retreat
- The awareness that you've been repeating the same relationship mistakes for years
- Persistent frustration and lack of peace

Not all of God's signs are enjoyable. Some are unpleasant or painful. But if that's what it takes to get your attention, it's worth it. Pay attention to the events and patterns in your life. Is God telling you to wait? If you haven't been listening, now is a good time to start. If not, you might squander time that you'll never get back.

DOES IT REALLY HAVE TO BE UNTIL MARRIAGE?

We faced a really tough question in writing this book:

Is The Wait only about waiting until marriage?

Yes. We do believe that most people's lives and relationships would be stronger and more joyful if they waited until marriage. On the other hand, many of the people reading this book, no matter how strong their faith, will probably have sex or continue to before marriage. To ignore that would not only be dismissive but could be viewed as borderline delusional. Just like you, we live in the real world where we try every day to live as spiritual beings dealing with the challenges of our flesh, so we do understand.

However, even with that understanding, we are confident that saving sex until after marriage will yield the best results, both for you as an individual and for you and your partner. That's what we did. We can speak to the blessings firsthand. We've seen God do amazing things in our lives that we believe are directly connected to putting him first in all areas of our life—including our sex life.

We get that some people's strong desire for sex and their differing perspectives on premarital sex might make them unlikely to wait until marriage. That said, we believe that to gain all the blessings connected to The Wait, celibacy should continue until you make that vow of lasting commitment. Not to say that God won't bless you if you choose to live differently, but since making our choice we've reaped the benefits of blessings that are nothing like we've ever received in our lives before.

Because we've written this book from that perspective, that's our focus. Plus, qualifying everything—different rules for people waiting for different lengths of time—would be confusing for you and us. So we're just going to talk about The Wait as we experienced it: no sex until marriage. We're not denying the real world; we're just reflecting on the way that the two of us navigated the real world and our own sexual desires to find real, deep, authentic love.

THE BLESSINGS OF WAITING

Despite all our reassurances and your best intentions, giving up sex can seem impossible. But believe us, it's worth it. The things that happened in the months after our marriage were not things we could have planned or even thought we deserved. We prayed for things and envisioned exactly how they would happen, but it wasn't until we were together— with the richness and respect that we had built for each other—that miracles began to come to pass. God's grace has been overwhelming and life changing. Putting God first and making him the foundation of our union has been not only the best personal decision we've ever made but the best decision for our careers and lives.

DEVON: When you're disciplined, obedient, and faithful, God will bring you the full manifestation of what He has in mind for you. He'll bring you His plan A, the best destiny you could imagine. That's what I wanted for my life when I became celibate. I knew that if I had remained undisciplined and continued to make bad choices, God would still be a benevolent God. He would bring me something from plan B, plan C, or plan D, but that wasn't enough for me. I said, "Lord, I want it all." And when you look at my life since then in all its facets, from family to career, God has delivered above and beyond anything I could have hoped or asked for.

MEAGAN: Everything in my life has changed dramatically since I stopped picking and choosing which parts of the Bible I would follow. I stopped saying, "I'm going to do *this* by the book, but I'm going to do *that* over there the way I want to do it." When I stopped that and I focused on the hardest thing, which is sex, I literally watched everything in my life and career change.

Waiting for sex isn't easy, but no important thing is ever easy. It's a sacrifice, but a worthwhile one. We took some teasing about things like our clear skin and how wild our honeymoon must have been, but it was worth it. Finally enjoying sex with each other after our marriage was incredible, but it was also the consummation of something holy.

WISE WAITING

Influential philosopher St. Thomas Aquinas said, "A person is said to be patient . . . because he acts in a praiseworthy manner by enduring things which hurt him here and now and is not unduly saddened by them." We consider patience a virtue and impatience a vice, but why?

In part, it's because a patient disposition tends to give us a healthier perspective on the ups and downs of daily living. Because we're not expecting everything to come our way overnight, we keep the big picture in mind. We're less likely to become angry or depressed at life's trivial setbacks. The impatient person can't understand why everything isn't working out as planned and is more likely to react to a minor misfortune by becoming frustrated, giving up, or doing something foolish.

CELIBACY VERSUS ABSTINENCE

Before we move on, we need to draw a clear distinction between celibacy and abstinence. Most people think they're the same thing. They're not. *Abstinence* is simply refraining from sex; it's the absence of something with no greater meaning behind it. To us, *Celibacy* is refraining from sex because of a vow or faith; it's abstinence with a purpose. You might abstain from sex involuntarily, because you're not in a relationship. Celibacy is never involuntary. It's always the result of a conscious, deliberate choice. That's an important distinction.

In *The Wait* we're going to talk about celibacy because to us, celibacy is something you go into with your eyes open, fully expecting to gain something from the experience. It's about saying, "I'm becoming." On the other hand, in our culture abstinence is something grudging, something forced upon young people, for example, by well-meaning parents or well-meaning ministries. It's about saying, "You will not." But there's not always purpose or learning associated with it. That can be dangerous.

Consider the news story in the spring of 2015 about a small high school in Texas with an abstinence-only sex education program that experienced a widespread outbreak of chlamydia, a sexually transmitted infection. That's one tiny piece of proof that just saying no to sex or pretending the sex drive doesn't exist isn't an adequate defense against pregnancy, disease, or worse.

When we talk about celibacy, the last thing we're doing is telling you to ignore sex. Just the opposite. We're suggesting that you acknowledge its power and your own desire. That way, if you choose to go without sex, you'll do so with your eyes open, understanding the realities and risks of having sex and *not* having it. Celibacy and The Wait complement each other.

THE ENERGY TO CHANGE EVERYTHING

Despite all those positives, type-A personalities often see The Wait as disempowering or fatalistic. So many times we hear self-help tropes like, "Go for what you want in life" and "Successful people make things happen; unsuccessful people watch things happen." That sort of one-size-fits-all wisdom sounds enticing until you realize that it could possibly leave God completely out of the picture.

For some scriptural perspective, look at Isaiah 40:30–31 (NASB), which reads,

> *Though youths grow weary and tired,*
> *And vigorous young men stumble badly,*
> *Yet those who wait for the LORD*
> *Will gain new strength;*
> *They will mount up with wings like eagles,*
> *They will run and not get tired,*
> *They will walk and not become weary.*

Yes, even those vigorous young men and women, so im-

patient and confident in their ability to choose the right person or right path, will stumble and wear out without God's
guidance to give them strength.

Running through love's maze, chasing one bad relationship after another—it all discourages not just the body but
also the spirit. The word *discourage* says it: a loss of courage.
After a while, you don't have the fortitude to face another
first date or relationship. It's exhausting.

On the other hand, showing some restraint and letting
God reveal your next step is like plugging into an emotional
and spiritual power plant. As the verse says, you can run and
not get tired. You're not just free of the maze but free of the
unspoken mandate that you must find your life's partner and
life's purpose right now. You're on nobody's schedule but
your own, and you have God to help you figure out what to
do next.

In fact, the same engine that drives the best stories also
gives The Wait its power. We're professionals with years
working in the entertainment business, and we know that
the key to any good movie is tension. It doesn't matter if
you're waiting for two characters to share their first kiss or
holding your breath while the heroine tries to escape from
the serial killer. No matter the genre of film, what moves the
story is the tension between what the main character wants
and the obstacles he or she must overcome to get it.

The Wait works the same way. It takes the tension that exists between instant and delayed gratification and turns it into energy. In the Bible, giving in to the temptations of instant gratification inevitably leads to ruin. (See Eden, Garden of.) Delayed gratification, on the other hand, leads to fidelity and reward. (See the story of Joseph.) Waiting for what you want floods your life with potential energy.

DELAYED GRATIFICATION AND MARSHMALLOWS

One memorable piece of evidence for the benefits of delayed gratification comes from what's become known as the famous Stanford marshmallow experiment. In the 1960s, a Stanford University professor named Walter Mischel started experimenting with hundreds of children around four and five years old to see how long they could delay their own gratification.

In the experiment, a researcher brought each child into a private room one at a time and sat down across a table from him or her. On the table he placed a marshmallow. Then he told each child that he would leave the room for fifteen minutes. If the child did not eat the marshmallow during the time that the researcher was gone, he or she would get a second marshmallow when the researcher came back. If the child ate the marshmallow, he or she wouldn't get any more.

As you might expect, most of the kids ate their marsh-mallows. A few didn't. But the interesting part of the study came as the researchers followed the kids over the next forty years as they grew into adults. What the study showed was that the kids who were able to delay gratification were more successful in almost every area of life: reduced rates of obe-sity, better social skills, higher SAT scores, you name it. They were simply better at life than the kids who gave in to instant gratification.

If you've never been disciplined enough to deny yourself short-term pleasure in favor of the big picture, The Wait is your chance to develop this skill as an adult, something most people cannot do. Doing so can increase your chances of being successful in the parts of your life that matter most, from your career to your relationships.

BEING SELECTIVE MAKES YOU MORE DESIRABLE

Another big plus to delaying gratification and reining in your dating life is that the less available you are, the more fascinat-ing you become. We live in a culture where most people hurl themselves blindly into the path of every possible relation-ship. In that world, who's most interesting and desirable?

The person who has the confidence not to date every warm body that comes along but instead is selective. Just as tension powers the action in the movies, it will do the same for you.

You may be dating and deciding to wait for the first time. You may be single and already waiting (on purpose or because you have no other choice) but becoming discouraged. Either way, have hope. The Wait will work for you. Ultimately, if your desire to please God is greater than your desire to please yourself (and even the person you may be dating), then God will bring you boundless blessings. Tether your will to wait to your desire to please God, and He will bless you and honor your commitment in ways that will surprise you and improve your life.

THE WAIT AND . . . CAREER

Your career is another area where you might be chomping at the bit to get going, get climbing that ladder, and get the corner office, but you have only so much control. There are politics, the realities of advancement within an organization, and issues of training and education to deal with. Plus, it's hard to know what you should really do with your life.

Waiting can be a great career strategy, because believe it or not God honors your sacrifice. And let's face it, the decision to deny yourself and not have sex is a sacrifice. The two of us have witnessed firsthand how God has blessed our careers because we chose to honor him in our relationship. As you practice The Wait, you can see a great acceleration and advancement in your purpose and career.

CHAPTER TWO

GETTING WHAT YOU REALLY WANT (HINT: IT ISN'T SEX)

Happiness is pleasure without regret.
—LEO TOLSTOY

Asking anyone to give up sex is asking a lot. We know that. We're asking you to shut down a fundamental part of what makes you human, and it's not easy.

Change is always difficult, which is why people so often retreat into the familiar even when the familiar is awful and depressing. That's why we get back together with our exes even if things ended the last time in screaming and broken glass. It's why we go out with the same friends even when we know they bring out the worst in us. We crave familiarity, and The Wait asks you to dive into unfamiliar territory. But that's what makes it such a powerful force for change.

BECOMING THE BEST VERSION OF YOURSELF

Millions of us are in pain. God designed sex and love to be a power combination in marriage. However, when sex and love don't end in marriage—which describes the outcome of most sexual flings and love affairs—the result is oftentimes painful. When you're with someone God doesn't intend for you, pain of some sort is usually inevitable.

Many of us still bear the wounds and the sorrow from those lost loves or flings. But do we give ourselves time to heal? No, not typically. Suffering from post-traumatic relationship disorder, we take the only prescription we know: we bury the feelings that we aren't ready to deal with, go into denial mode, and look for escape in other sexual relationships. But we need time to really process the pain we've gone through and properly heal so that we don't make the same mistakes again. Reason number one to practice The Wait: it's a time to heal when the only one who matters is you.

Celibacy is the heart and soul of The Wait because control over this area of instant gratification empowers you to have control over so many other areas in your life—the same ones that may have led to a repetitive pattern of heartbreak, loneliness, wasted money, and wasted time.

When we base our actions on that "I-want-what-I-want-when-I-want-it" drive, we don't see clearly. We make decisions based on lust, greed, envy, or fear, and more often than not such choices cause destruction in our lives. Sometimes the harm is temporary, as in a bad breakup that's painful for a few weeks but survivable. Other times the damage is permanent, such as when quick decisions results in disease, depression, or an unplanned pregnancy and changes the course of our lives forever.

Speaking of disease, we'd be remiss if we didn't highlight the serious problem of Sexually Transmitted Diseases (STDs):

- Both young men and young women are heavily affected by STDs—but young women face the most serious long-term health consequences. It is estimated that undiagnosed STDs cause 24,000 women to become infertile each year. —*Center for Disease Control, December 2014*
- African Americans are the racial/ethnic group most affected by HIV. —*Center for Disease Control, HIV/AIDS*
- The rate of new HIV infection in African Americans is 8 times that of whites based on population size. —*Center for Disease Control, HIV/AIDS*
- African Americans accounted for an estimated 44% of all new HIV infections among adults and adolescents (aged 13 years or older) in 2010, despite representing

only 12% of the US population; considering the smaller size of the African American population in the United States, this represents a population rate that is 8 times that of whites overall. —*Center for Disease Control, HIV/AIDS*

- In 2010, African American women accounted for 6,100 (29%) of the estimated new HIV infections among all adult and adolescent African Americans. This number represents a decrease of 21% since 2008. Most new HIV infections among African American women (87%; 5,300) are attributed to heterosexual contact. The estimated rate of new HIV infections for African American women (38.1/100,000 population) was 20 times that of white women and almost 5 times that of Hispanic/ Latino women. —*Center for Disease Control, HIV/AIDS*

When we're focused primarily on satisfying our immediate desires, we're preventing ourselves from being the best people we can be. And one of the key elements of being the best people we can be is to be the healthiest person we can be. The short-term results of instant gratification might be fun, but in the long term we often damage our health and ourselves. Not to mention we can become like addicts chasing the next high. The Wait helps put reason and discernment back in charge.

But it doesn't stop there. Waiting for sex is a powerful

tool for taking control of our impulses and creating positive habits. The Wait applies to every area of romantic life and relationships, from whom we choose to date to when to get serious. In all these areas, people tend to try to *make* things happen. We force the issue. We delude ourselves into thinking that we alone can order the universe to our liking if we just have the right look, income, or position.

The Wait reminds us that while we have the power of choice, much of what happens in our life is still subject to God's control. Our hands are on the wheel, but so are God's. We can steer with him, because we do have control over our choices, our habits, and how we use the gifts we've been given. But if we try to take over, we usually find ourselves in a head-on collision with something or someone that God was trying to steer us away from.

Practicing The Wait is a chance to heal, clear your head, do some important self-assessment, and position yourself to receive peace, love, and wisdom. It's an opportunity to take a break from the frantic feeling that you have to make things happen or they won't happen at all. The Wait is about having faith that God is working on your behalf to bring you the right blessings at the right time. It's also about recognizing that all the time you spend or have spent chasing booty actually works against you and your desire to improve yourself in body, mind, and spirit.

The Wait is that critical period between *wanting* and *getting*. It's when you quiet your mind and trust God. Relieved of the pressure to live the perfect life (whew!), you're free to reinvent yourself as the person you've always aspired to be—the person He intends you to be. For some people, that means taking classes and working out. For others, it means reading Scripture and ridding themselves of toxic relationships. While waiting, you need to trust more than ever before that God's got your back, then start making choices for your life that show you have your own back, too.

Even for people with strong faith, this isn't always easy. We ache to find our life partners, to find that person who can fall in love with us and be loved by us. So we push the issue. We date everyone attractive who crosses our path without employing some critical thinking or prayer to help us determine if this is someone worthy of our time. We stay in relationships that are way past their sell-by date. We say yes to quick marriages and then end up saying yes to quick divorces. It's not making us any happier. It's not making us any wealthier. In fact, it's making us more cynical, and sometimes loading us up with heavy emotional baggage that we'll need to unpack years down the road.

In the midst of all this pain and frustration, we can begin to think that finding real love isn't possible. Maybe settling for a series of hookups is the best we can hope for from life.

However, cynicism doesn't stop us from yearning desperately for something more, for connection to each other and to God. We don't have to give in to cynicism.

Sometimes, you can't find what you desire most.
Sometimes, it has to find YOU.

The Wait is one of the most powerful tools you'll ever have for getting what you really want out of life because it creates the path for you to become the best version of yourself. When this happens, getting what you want most out of life—the love of your life, a wonderful family, a prosperous career, and a meaningful life's purpose—becomes truly possible. You grow into someone of greater wisdom, discernment, self-awareness, compassion, and empathy, and it's incredible how everything falls into place. It's as though God was always just around the corner, waiting to bless you when you found your way onto the right path.

BEFORE WE DATED

When the two of us met in 2007, we may not have felt anxiety over how our lives were progressing, but we didn't grasp the significance of what God was doing, either. We were just two people in the entertainment industry, and we both thought that we had a pretty good handle on what was coming our way.

God knew better. He was bringing us together carefully, and it took us both a while to acknowledge that there was more going on than we could grasp. But in due time, we both had an idea that something bigger might be at work.

MEAGAN: I'm passionate about doing films with a spiritual heartbeat. I did this independent film called *Miles from Home*, about a kid who ends up on the street because his mother is strung out on drugs and his father's not in the picture. My character was quirky and offbeat and a strong Christian. She meets this kid and doesn't know that he's fallen into the world of prostitution, and they fall in love. By the end of the film, he chooses life. He decides to stop going down a path of destruction and be with this girl.

DeVon saw the film and said, "Wow, I didn't know she was such a good actress." Around this same time a mutual friend of ours, Benji, was trying to set up a general meeting for me with DeVon. DeVon spoke with Evan, my manager, about the meeting; he was excited to meet me because he had just seen *Miles from Home*. I'll never forget when I first walked in. Immediately I thought he was very attractive, but I had a boyfriend at the time. We had a great meeting and he was enthusiastic about helping me with my career. He said, "Whatever you need, I'm on your team," and that was the beginning of our friendship.

DEVON: Fast-forward to December 2009. Meagan had made a lot of movies for Sony because Clint Culpepper, the head of Screen Gems, a division of Sony Pictures, really liked her. She was on the Sony Pictures lot (the same lot I worked on) quite often to go to meetings, recording dialogue for films like *Stomp the Yard*, things like that. One day, I just happened to be on the lot on Main Street when she came by in the golf cart that security uses to take talent around. As she was driving by, she asked me to jump on, and on the way to the parking lot she told me about a new trailer for a new movie she had just finished producing and starring in called *Video Girl*. I told her I'd love to see it, so Lee, the guy driving the cart, dropped us at her car and she gave me the DVD.

Part of me was thinking, "Wow, this is Meagan Good, I can't believe it! This is cool!" But another part of me was saying, "No, don't let your mind go there, this is not reality." I took the trailer from her and she left. Later on I watched the trailer and liked it. I sent it back to her along with an email about how much I enjoyed it, and then that was it. We didn't have any more interaction until over a year later when we started casting *Jumping the Broom*.

Starting with being on location for *Jumping the Broom* (the first chance we'd had to spend substantial time together) it was clear to both of us that maybe there was a spark and some chemistry between us. But there were also all manner of doubts, thought processes, and obstacles that neither of us could have known the other was dealing with. So if, instead of paying full attention to God's direction and biding our time, we had surrendered to the attraction and jumped into an on-location romance, what would have happened? The odds are we wouldn't be married today.

MEAGAN: I was in the fourth year of a relationship that had become destructive. I had been praying, "Lord, what do you want me to do? I want to be with this person, but things are emotionally abusive and dysfunctional on both sides. Am I supposed to stick it out and hope things get better?"

The Lord told me, "Just wait."

Shortly after that, I went off to start filming *Jumping the Broom* in Nova Scotia. I would see DeVon on the set and think, "That's the type of guy I wish I could be with. He has a great heart, he's funny, and he loves the Lord." Right off the bat, I felt like we were kindred spirits. But we kept it strictly platonic and professional. After I left, I felt in my spirit it was time to end the relationship I was in. Then I said to the Lord, "Okay, now what?"

The Lord answered, "Work on yourself."

Well, it wasn't pretty. For the next few months, I was self-destructive: drinking, partying hard, and angry that I had spent so much time in a toxic situation. I wasn't in a good space; I needed time to heal. I definitely wasn't thinking about getting into another relationship.

DEVON: When I met Meagan, I was already in a relation-ship. Funny as it sounds to say now, I also didn't want to date an actress. I just didn't think it would be the right life and career fit.

When we started work on *Jumping the Broom*, she was one of the first people at the hotel when I checked in. While we were downstairs in the lobby making small talk, I saw a cigarette in her hand. She had a toothbrush with her, too, because she didn't want the smoking to stain her teeth. I was floored. I was thinking, "How in the world can someone this beautiful be a smoker?"

Later, I would find out that she also liked to drink

(like, really drink). I don't drink, but I'd dated people who drank. However, I had never dated anyone who smoked. But it wasn't my worry because at the time I wasn't thinking about us ever dating; we just had a good professional relationship. So while we hung out on the set and went out a few times with the cast and crew, we were cordial and that was all. I knew there was a lot going on with her, but I didn't know anything about her relationship outside of what was in the press. Eventually, after the movie wrapped, I went back to L.A. and that was that.

As far as we were concerned, we were both making prudent decisions based on the circumstances in our lives. But with God, nothing is ever that simple. Making sure that each of us ends up with the people we are meant to be with is important to the Lord, so He takes His time making sure that the circumstances are right. We had no idea at the time that by just living our lives and doing our best to honor our commitments, God was putting us on a love collision course.

On our own, we both discovered something crucial: only by deliberately refusing to repeat past relationship mistakes could we gain the clarity and perspective we needed to understand what we wanted, what we needed to do differently, and what God had in mind for us. Choosing to steer clear of personal entanglement in favor of personal growth gave us both what we needed to come together when we were truly ready and create something that's been blessed and amazing.

WISE WAITING

Some of the world's greatest success stories are about people who knew that nothing they did could influence events in their favor, so they chose to wait for conditions to shift.

One of the best examples from Scripture is the story of the Exodus, when God liberated the Hebrews from slavery. Unable to match the might of the Egyptians, Moses had to wait years for conditions to change and for God to ordain the right time to bring about change.

In *The Art of War*, Sun Tzu wrote about the power of patience in allowing the opposition to defeat itself: "He who is prudent and lies in wait for an enemy who is not, will be victorious."

When no action other than preparation will deliver the result you're striving for, being patient and allowing conditions to change can get the best results. There are times to take aggressive action yet they will usually be preceded by a strong period of waiting.

HOW THE WAIT IMPROVED OUR LIVES

Even back then, though we hadn't yet developed the concept of The Wait, we were practicing its precepts. We were more concerned with being obedient to God than with following some temporary blip of sexual excitement. We were questioning and cautious about each other, resolving to watch and see what would happen next. We were very aware of the mistakes we had made in past relationships and determined not to repeat them. So we played it cool. We didn't let our interest distract us from bigger things in our lives at the time.

That pattern would play out over and over as we kept circling each other. Circumstances would force us into proximity with each other, where our raw chemistry and interest in each other's personality and intelligence would flow. But we kept backing off, listening to God and saying, "Wait. Let's see how this plays out."

Obviously, this approach paid big rewards. Our marriage is a powerful, mutually respectful relationship. Many people we meet ask us time and again for our secret to happiness. We know how very much God has blessed us, but that wouldn't have happened without The Wait. Practicing it has improved our lives in more ways than we can count:

We're more patient. We've always been ambitious people, but our experience waiting and watching God bring us together has taught us the incredible virtue of patience. There are some things that we can't make happen. Other things will happen, but only in their own time when certain conditions have been met. We're sure of that now, and our greater patience has helped us land the right career opportunities, wait for the right time to buy a house, and so much more. We feel like we see a big picture of blessings that are available to everybody, but not everybody takes time to see it.

We're free to be ourselves. Dating is like putting on your church clothes, and if you don't ever let someone know your less-than-perfect side before you get married, you could spend your entire life wearing those clothes, afraid to be yourself. We're not worried about that. We practiced The Wait learning about each other in every way. We spent more time on dates talking about what we liked, didn't like, were offended by, you name it. We've seen each other at our weirdest, silliest, most ornery and disagreeable, most vulnerable, and most hurtful. And guess what? We've both made the decision to love the whole package. That means we both have a safe space where we can be ourselves without judgment. It's a wonderful space to live in.

We have a home within a home. We both can work incredibly long hours in demanding professions. Whether you're acting or producing, shooting a film or television show can mean months of fourteen-hour days on location. That means one of us—and sometimes both of us—is often coming home drained utterly dry. Don't get us wrong; we know how blessed we are to do what we do. But it can be exhausting.

And when our wells are dry, we have each other to fill them up. We have someplace to go and someone to go to that is ours, our haven, our center of peace. Home is about the person more than the place. Our marriage is our home, and it fills us back up when the world drains us.

We've made peace with the past. Meagan in particular had some demons from her past relationships, but we both bore scars from breakups and poor choices. The worst thing about past pain is that it makes you doubt your wisdom to make sound choices. As we confronted our demons, we decided to let go of the guilt of previous mistakes we've made in relationships. We decided not to allow our past to control our future. And practicing The Wait helped us release a lot of baggage.

THE WAIT AND . . . FINANCES

Oh, that crazy consumer culture. We fuel a trillion-dollar economy because we just can't help instantly gratifying our insatiable desires for new cars, shoes, and flat-screen televisions the size of NYC. It's no wonder that Americans save only a small percentage of our incomes.

Waiting is a powerful principle when it comes to your money—more to the point, to spending less of it and saving more. If you follow the precepts it's pretty simple: don't give in to your hunger for a shiny new toy. Save that money instead for the purchases that will provide for your future, like a home, an IRA, or 401(k). Or just stick it in a savings account so that in five years you can take your Wait-met spouse on the honeymoon of a lifetime.

There's nothing too complicated here. The Wait and money means focusing on long-term versus short-term goals. Want to buy a house? Saving is a must. That doesn't mean you can't still eat out and have nice things, but you might have to do that more selectively than before. Decide what's important and manage your money accordingly.

GRABBING HOLD OF THE LIFE YOU WANT

One of the most important reasons people choose to delay gratification is also the simplest: *it helps us get what we want.* Successful dieters resist the temptation to overeat because they like seeing a slimmer reflection, not because they love watching what they eat all day long. People who sacrifice to save cushy retirement nest eggs do it mostly because they want to have money in their older years, not because they don't have a desire to spend money. Our desires are powerful drivers of our decision-making process, which helps or hinders us from getting what we want most.

The two of us are not naive. The promise of becoming the person God wants you to be isn't necessarily enough to change behavior by itself, particularly when it comes to love and sex, areas where we humans are prone to stepping on our own toes. If you want to wait to date, have sex, get married, or do anything else purely out of deep religious or moral conviction, we admire and respect that. But the desire to wait is different from the ability to wait, and it's a lot easier to remain celibate and delay gratification if you know you're doing it because it brings concrete benefits.

THE WAIT REPROGRAMS YOUR PLEASURE SOFTWARE

Psychologists, anthropologists, and others have studied self-control and delayed gratification for years. They've found that the ability to say no to immediate, short-term pleasures in favor of lasting ones down the line is linked to better mental and physical health, greater academic success, and more refined social abilities. Several leading clinical psychologists call self-control the "master virtue" because people who exhibit a high degree of it also feel better, have higher self-esteem, and deal with anger and other negative feelings more productively.

Why does delaying gratification make us better people? Sigmund Freud pointed to the ego's ability to strike a bargain between the id (the "let's get it on" part of the mind) and the superego (the center of principle and morality). But that still doesn't explain the reason why The Wait is such a powerful tool for getting what you want.

We believe we have the answer, and it's all about how our minds and bodies are programmed to see pleasure. Every day is a contest between pleasures of the flesh and of the spirit. Fleshly pleasures are about immediate satisfaction of our desires through things like food, sex, spending money, feeling superior to other people, and so on. We call these pleasures SEE: Short-Term, External Experiences.

You might have noticed that SEE have a lot in common with addictive behaviors. People get addicted to spending money, gambling, sex, and food. These quick-fix experiences that give us instant gratification can also control our behavior and lead us into destructive choices.

Spiritual pleasures, on the other hand, evoke our highest qualities, the ones that move us to do the will of God and align with who He wants us to be. Generosity, discipline, fidelity, compassion, self-sacrifice, acting ethically and honestly—these are some of the pleasures that we call LIP: Long-Term, Internal Processes. Cultivating these qualities often means delaying gratification and waiting for results; for example, it can take months to see the weight loss that comes from being disciplined about exercise and diet. The process affects us mostly in our minds and spirits and leads to positive change and personal growth. When we do the right thing or care for others before ourselves, we get a soul-deep sense of pleasure and accomplishment that's nothing like the superficial pleasures of the flesh.

Emotionally and spiritually healthy people maintain a good balance between fleshly and spiritual pleasures. They date widely but don't sleep around. They enjoy material comforts but don't overspend. They live balanced lives by putting God first and still finding ways to enjoy the blessings God has placed in this world. The trouble is, our culture works 24-7 to tell us that fleshly pleasure (instant gratification) is the better way to live. Companies make billions of dollars convincing us that we need—no, deserve—food, music, sex, new clothing, high-end technology, and incredible experiences all the time. We've become programmed to favor the flesh over the spirit.

This harms us in more ways than we can count. The continuous, unbalanced practice of choosing short-term pleasures blinds us, corrupts our willpower, and drives choices that ultimately can destroy our lives. For example, we have unprotected sex with people we barely know, abuse alcohol or drugs and call it fun, stay in dysfunctional relationships and call it love, and spend more money than we have and call it prosperity. In a nutshell, choosing the flesh over the spirit can be dangerously self-destructive.

In Scripture, it says:

> *"Those who live according to the flesh have their minds set on what the flesh desires; but those who live in accordance with the Spirit have their minds set on what the Spirit desires. The mind governed by the flesh is death, but the mind governed by the Spirit is life and peace. The mind governed by the flesh is hostile to God; it does not submit to God's law, nor can it do so. Those who are in the realm of the flesh cannot please God."*

(ROMANS 8:5–8, NIV)

The greatest benefit of The Wait is that it reprograms us to find greater pleasure in choices that help us live according to the Spirit—that is, aligning our spirit with God's. This serves our long-term mental, emotional, and spiritual health. Take us as an example. By choosing to wait and not pursue a physical relationship before marriage, we were able to appreciate the pleasure that came with listening to God, learning about ourselves, and breaking old patterns. The current success we experience in our marriage is directly related to the years we spent individually trying to find the balance between the flesh and the spirit.

When you choose to deny the flesh in favor of the spirit you'll be surprised to find that doing things in this way feels really good—and that giving in to the needs of the flesh starts to feel less desirable. Even better, the more you derive pleasure from spirit-led decisions that make you stronger and more self-aware, the better choices you'll make in your personal and professional life. You'll get off the treadmill of past mistakes and get on the elliptical of current and future success. You'll take big strides toward becoming the person you've always wanted to be.

LIP SERVICE

The essence of The Wait is developing the ability to derive more pleasure and peace from delaying gratification than you do from giving in to the hunger for instant gratification. By encouraging your spiritual development you will make choices that reward you over the long term and improve your happiness in every area of your life.

What kind of choices can bring you greater pleasure and satisfaction than quick-fix pleasures of the flesh? Here are some examples:

- Maintaining a disciplined program of fitness
- Budgeting and saving money
- Praying and meditating consistently
- Being celibate, which eliminates distractions and improves vision, clarity, and discernment
- Helping others in need
- Mentoring and giving back
- Finding a church community that can help nurture you and give you support

Anytime you act with morality, restraint, good character, or strong discipline—when you do things that enhance instead of corrupt your spirit—you will enjoy tremendous peace, pride, and

personal satisfaction. That's the kind of pleasure that lasts . . . and
will fuel long-term success.

IT PUTS YOU BACK IN CONTROL

Every time you give yourself to someone before marriage,
you give them your power. It's time to take your power back.
It's time to take control of your decisions, which is where the
real power lies.

Many times, the waiting periods in life come to us not
by our own choice. Circumstances like a breakup or job loss
force them on us. Instead of using these periods as opportunities to do the work we've needed to do, we use these periods
to complain, throw a self-pity party, and spiral into depression. One of the many goals of The Wait is to motivate you
to change your thinking about unexpected seasons—to use
periods of active waiting to sculpt your life into the shape you
want.

It's true that God is the only one who knows the right
time for a person or opportunity to appear in your life. However, you have control over how you prepare before that
person or opportunity arrives—and how you respond afterward. God gives us all the raw material we will ever need to
become the person He wants us to become, but it's up to us to

do the cutting and polishing so that the true beauty and light of our character and God-intended destiny emerges.

With The Wait, you can accelerate the process of growth and attract good outcomes into your life by taking control of your choices. Of course, this also means that you must resist the temptation to sit around and complain that God isn't blessing you. That's a deadly trap that will deplete your energy and divert your focus. Complaining is a liability to be avoided at all costs. From the perspective of The Wait, the time when nothing appears to be happening becomes your personal self-development laboratory. You can prepare for things to come, asking key questions and reflecting on what you've done wrong in the past so you can do things right in the future. It's the time to ask some of the most challenging questions you'll ever confront:

- What's likely to happen and how can I be ready?
- What part did I play in the failure of my last relationship or opportunity?
- What negative patterns do I see myself repeating over and over?
- Am I pursuing opportunities that please my flesh over my spirit?
- What type am I attracted to? Am I attracted to people who aren't right for me?

- What emotions have sabotaged my relationships? Rage? Depression? Revenge?
- What traumas have I not worked through yet? Betrayal?

Evaluating your traumatic relationship ups and downs productively is constructive action. Set aside the victim mentality, which makes you believe you are the victim of your past relationships gone wrong. It does nothing but rob you of control and of the privilege of taking responsibility for your part. Take your power back. By doing what needs to be done to avoid past mistakes (change your cell number, join a new gym, take an overdue vacation to clear your head, whatever) you prepare yourself for the incredible future God has in store for you.

MEAGAN: Actively deciding to wait was not about me finding my guy. It was about the fact that some of the relationships I had been in were destructive to who I was as a human being, and to who I wanted to be in God. I played a huge role in this as well. I knew better. Everything was in disarray, and I needed to let God put the pieces back together. It was time for me to not be stagnant in my growth and to choose to take my relationship with God deeper and closer.

DEVON: When we're distracted by our drama, we're not doing the work that God is calling us to do. We're not giving

Him what he needs to make things happen. For instance, I couldn't make *Jumping the Broom* come to be on my own, but I could open myself to God's hand on my life. So I looked for projects with a larger purpose behind them. When *Jumping the Broom* came along, I said, "There's something about this film. I'm going to do what I can to get it made."

I didn't worry that I would only have a small budget to make the film. I approached the opportunity from a place of faith and obedience to God, and with the belief that making this movie was key to my preparation to one day become a producer. I had no idea that God would ultimately use the film to set up and prepare me for my life with Meagan.

There's great power in cooling down, stepping back, looking at things with a clear head, and most important, breaking the cycle of repeated mistakes. You gain the perspective to make preparations that will lead to the outcomes you want, and you gain control during periods of life that might seem uncontrollable.

IT PULLS THE RIGHT PEOPLE TO YOU

Self-control won't do much for you if everyone around you lacks it. In Philippians 2: 1–2 (NASB), Scripture reads, "*If there is any consolation of love, if there is any fellowship of the Spirit, if any affection and compassion, make my joy complete by being of the same mind, maintaining the same love, united in spirit, intent on one purpose.*" Achieving joy and fulfillment means surrounding yourself with like-minded people.

Ultimately, having such people in your life becomes very important to helping you reach your goals. It's tough to live according to your faith—to be celibate and desire to live a strong Christian life, for example—when everyone else in your immediate social circle isn't committed to doing the same. Those friends won't just tempt you to fall off the delayed-gratification wagon; they'll also take up room in your life that God might be reserving for people more like you.

A key benefit of The Wait is that it attracts those people—people who share your ability to find pleasure in patience. Like it or not, you are who you hang with, and that's especially true when you're defying cultural norms. When you decide that you're going to be the one person in your circle who doesn't chase sex like dogs chase cars, you'll be pressured to conform. Most people are acutely aware of their harmful behavior patterns and dependence on instant gratification; however, to make themselves feel better, they'll try to get you to do the same. It's easier to resist that pressure when you're not doing it alone.

Our marriage is proof that God can and will bring like-minded people together. Neither of us had a clue that the other was going through a preparation process that would ultimately lead us to each other, but that didn't matter. We both chose to opt out of the pursuit of dating traps that had failed us in the past in favor of the pursuit of wholeness, and when it was time and we were ready, God brought us together.

Like attracts like; it's a law of human nature. Practicing The Wait can be lonely in our "God grant me patience and I want it now" society. If you stay constant in your determination to do things the right way, you'll be surprised by how God will bring the right, healthy people into your life. They'll flock to you for leadership, camaraderie, love, and support. The right group of friends helps you grow individually and collectively. And who knows—one of the people you attract might be just the person you were meant to be with.

OTHER KEY REASONS WHY WAITING IS WORTH IT

Waiting reduces your risks. As mentioned before, premarital sex can lead to some nasty outcomes, from sexually transmitted infections to babies you're not ready for. Obviously, if you abstain from sexual activity, you reduce that risk to approximately zero.

Waiting reveals who your friends are. People are going to go all "OMG!" when you spill that you're giving up sex for a while. But your real friends, the ones who want the best for you, will get behind The Wait and support you through it. The people who aren't true friends will ridicule you at best, and try to sabotage you at worst. Great. Now you know who to put on hold from your life.

Waiting reveals your "triggers." Triggers are people, circumstances, or situations that weaken your ability to maintain your commitment to practicing The Wait. They whisper things like, "Hurry, all your best friends are married. What's wrong with you?" Practicing The Wait gives you an opportunity to see your triggers, which will empower you to not give in to them.

Waiting helps you think clearly. Sex clouds judgment and gives rise to self-delusions. One of the big reasons our relationship is so strong today is that when we were dating, we couldn't fall back on sex when talking got tough. When you're seeking God and you're focused on whatever you're supposed to be doing, you see yourself and the other person clearly. Our intimacy was about conversation, connection, friendship, and falling in love with each other without it having to be about sex.

Waiting honors God's timing and methods. The way God brings you a person can be as important as the person. It's important to have clarity of thought so you can see how God does what He does. God's hand bringing people into your life under the right circumstances at the right time helps strengthen your relationship with each other and the Lord. Imagine if God brought someone into your life at a time when you weren't ready or couldn't appreciate that person. You might never get together with the one who was meant for you because you weren't ready to give them a chance.

Waiting helps you choose people because you like them and feel a connection with them. You won't waste time with someone with whom you have nothing in common just because you want to get him or her into bed. Without sex as a go-to, you'll walk right past those people and choose to spend time with people whose character, intelligence, wit, and love for God you find irresistible.

Waiting reduces drama, conflict, and expense. How much cash do we burn to look sexy for people who don't even care? How much mental energy do we spend to wine and dine someone with the sole purpose of getting them into bed, only to discover later that they just wanted to get us in bed? Then there's the post-sex conflict, expectations, and crises. Giving up sex spares you this. Apart from the money, who wouldn't love to say good-bye to the walks of shame, morning-after scenes, waiting on the call that doesn't come, and feelings of being used?

Waiting gives you better knowledge of your partner. When you're not blinded by lust or the counterfeit intimacy that can come with premarital sex, you can see the person you're dating for who they are. You'll be less likely to rationalize their character flaws only to find yourself married to a stranger a few years later. That's important: one 2012 survey found that about six million Americans had concealed financial accounts from spouses or partners. That's financial infidelity. Wouldn't you want to know if you were considering committing to a person who was capable of that . . . before committing?

Waiting leads to better self-esteem. Is your partner with you mostly because the sex rocks their world? That's a problem, because sexual heat inevitably cools. If your significant other is with you only because of what happens between the sheets, you'll feel bad about yourself and might do some desperate things to keep him or her interested. Without sex in the picture, you know that your partner is with you for you.

Waiting will make your engagement a time of clarity. Celibacy brought the finish line for our courtship into clear focus. With sex on the sidelines, we were able to turn all our attention to the big questions. Did we share the same love of God? Did we want the same things? Were our tastes, interests, goals, and intellects compatible? When we decided that each answer was yes, we got engaged. With sex clouding the issues, getting to a proposal could take years.

Waiting will help you choose God's plan A. One of the big benefits of The Wait is that it lets you step out of the mad rush of dating and sex and expectations, giving you space and time to discover who you are and who you can become. That allows God to fully bless you with the clarity of your life's purpose. We're not saying that He *won't* bless you with purpose if you have premarital sex, but we believe there's a deeper level of clarity to be achieved when you don't.

Choose The Wait and retake control of your future. Instead of feeling resentful and angry about waiting for the love of your life, make the decision to take steps to fulfill the potential that God has placed in you. There's nothing disempowering about becoming God's collaborator in properly matching yourself with the life you deeply desire.

KNOW YOUR TRIGGERS

A trigger is anything that flips the panic switch in your brain and drives you to make reckless decisions. Knowing your triggers can help you either avoid them or learn to overcome the impulses that they provoke.

These are common triggers that seem to push most of us into bad relationships at one time or another:

- A friend or family member getting married
- Hitting an important birthday—turning thirty, for example
- A bad breakup
- The death of someone you know, especially someone close to you in age
- A life crisis such as divorce or job loss
- A crisis in your faith, such as doubting that God exists or has a plan for you

How many of these have you experienced? Did they trigger hasty or imprudent action that you regretted later? Start writing down the specific events, people, or circumstances that act as triggers for you. The clearer you are about them, the less they'll control you.

CHAPTER THREE

FIRST STEPS DOWN THE PATH TO AUTHENTIC LOVE

*Civilized people cannot fully satisfy
their sexual instinct without love.*
—BERTRAND RUSSELL

If you think of your life as a fight movie, then The Wait is like the training sequence. It's when the heroes train harder than they ever have before. They use discipline, hard work, and perseverance to prepare them for the fight of their lives. In the movie of your life, think of your training methods as prayer, meditation, working out, eating right, studying, growing, creating, seeking healthy relationships, and healing from negative ones. This is how you'll become the hero you're destined to be. During this period of time, do whatever you need to do to fulfill the great potential that God has placed in you. There's nothing passive about this. Quite the opposite, in fact. We can't think of a better strategy for getting what your heart desires than to become the kind of man or woman whose character attracts terrific people and whose skills and wisdom are the equal of any opportunity.

You might feel like you're already making steady progress toward becoming that person but could use a boost to get to the next level. On the other hand, maybe you're sick of being heartbroken and disappointed when it appears like everything good in your life turns out to be a disappointment.

MAKE THE DECISION

There's no magic to The Wait. You just have to make the commitment and stick to it. First, acknowledge the power of your sex drive and that it's okay. You want sex. You want it a lot. You think about it. You fantasize. We all do. It's fine. There's nothing wrong or sinful about that. But what are you compromising to have sex? What is sex costing you? What are you not experiencing in your life that you might find if you stop obeying your sex drive and start obeying the Lord?

Once you've answered those questions, there's a still more important one to answer. Can you make doing what's right more important than doing what feels good? We were both able to be celibate independently because we arrived at a mental and spiritual place where following the Word and allowing God to work in our lives was more important than any short-term pleasure. If you're at that point, then you're ready to try it.

If not, it's better to admit that you're not ready for The Wait. Just know that if you keep living the way you've been living, you'll keep getting the same results. You'll know when you've had enough and you're ready to try it.

Also know that when you tell potential partners about your wait, some will want nothing to do with it. That's a sacrifice you must be willing to make. In the long run, being able to bypass relationships with people who don't want the same things you want out of life is a blessing. It was a blessing that when we started dating, we were both celibate, but that's rare. More likely, you'll meet someone fascinating, and before too much time passes you'll tell him or her that you're celibate. Be clear about your motives: your love of God and your desire to be a better person and have a better life. Some will laugh in your face. Some will get angry. It will be obvious when you find a person who shares your values and goals.

Another question we hear a lot is, "What happens if I'm waiting and I wind up having sex anyway?" Well, when you're dieting and you give in to your craving for a large piece of chocolate cake, do you throw up your hands and say, "Whatever, I'm going to order a hot fudge sundae"? (Well, some do. But you shouldn't.) You should forgive yourself and get back on the horse. It's the same with sex. You're human. Talk it out with your partner and figure out how to keep the same thing from happening again.

SEEK WISE COUNSEL

When you're beginning The Wait, it's a good idea to seek some counseling, either from a relationship or spiritual counselor. Talk with someone who can help you figure out what baggage you're clinging to, where it comes from, and how to let it go. This can happen quickly, but the length of time doesn't really matter. What matters is getting a spring cleaning of your spirit that lets you go into the world clear-eyed and ready to approach dating and relationships in a new, healthy way.

LET GOD BE YOUR MATCHMAKER

What we didn't see then (but see clearly now) is that God was guiding us in the direction that He knew was best for us, and what was best for us was to come together when the Lord knew we were ready. God is at the heart of The Wait, but His role isn't always clear. Let's talk about it and we'll try to make it clear.

In trying to force the action in your life, you can easily overlook the fact that you're not the matchmaker of your life. God is. God has a way of matching us with the opportunities that align with His divine plan. While the items on your to-do list—get the great job, find the perfect apartment, get those six-pack abs—are important, they aren't to be done as if God doesn't have a plan for your life, including your love life. God already has the right life and relationship in mind for you. It may not be with the type of person you have in mind, and it may not be under the circumstances that you think are most desirable. But God knows how to make the perfect match if we allow him to match us.

The catch to this matchmaking is free will. We can ignore God's intentions for our lives if we want to; many people do. He's not going to force us to choose to live according to His will. It *has* to be our choice, because coerced change isn't change at all. It's punishment. However, God will put signs and symbols in our path—people, events, opportunities—that can show us the path in life that leads to joy and fulfillment. Then it's up to us to decide if we want to humble ourselves and submit to His plan, even if it seems to lead us away from what we want most.

If you've failed to choose God's will for your life, even

multiple times, you know what? There's nothing wrong with you. You might make some bad choices, have issues to work out, or be desperate to update your social media status to "In a Relationship," but that just means you're human. We're all human. All the relationship fails, bouts of loneliness, and romantic twists that seem like they're straight out of a romance novel . . . God can use all of this to help match you with the right person and the life he's always wanted you to have.

WHAT IF THE OTHER PERSON IS WAITING FIRST?

It's wise to prepare for people's reactions when you tell them that you're celibate. But what happens when the person you're on a second date with tells you that they're celibate? If you came to The Wait because someone you like asked you to forgo sex, does it mean as much as it does when it's your idea?

Of course it does. You're still making a choice to wait. You're not choosing celibacy with some ill-defined personal goal in mind. You're choosing it because you are saying to yourself, "I like this person and I'm going to do whatever it takes to be with them."

When someone else shares their celibacy commitment with you, be as open and respectful as you would like them to be with you. Ask lots of questions, share your faith, and if it seems like you two might be a good fit, suggest that you explore celibacy together. Any path into The Wait is a good one if it brings you to the destiny God has in mind for you.

GIVE UP THE ILLUSION OF "THE ONE"

When we start talking about God and God's will, some people leap to the idea of "the One," and that can be problematic.

It's a deeply romantic notion that there's one perfect person, a soul mate, for you somewhere in the world, and you're drawing inexorably closer to each other. The truth, however, is more complicated.

Let's be honest: most of us aren't interested in being patient. What we really want is to find the One right now. If we happen to be patient, it's begrudgingly, because there are no other available options. So we're patient by default. Meanwhile, we work hard to assemble the elements of a great life that leaves nothing to chance:

- Move to a city that's good for singles? Check.
- Work out and get fit? Check.
- Make sure what we wear, drive, and eat all make us look like a great catch? Triple check.

As far as we're concerned, we're going to climb the mountain, get the promotion, and make a lot of money. Then, like a film where the director just shouted "Action!" our perfect life partner will walk through the door at a party.

Of course, you should make yourself as desirable as possible and put yourself in the position to meet quality single people. That's just common sense. But problems begin when you believe that you can order a life partner the way you order a pizza: "Yes, I'd like a man who loves the Lord, six foot two, brown eyes, with a BMW and a six-pack, please." Or, "I'd like a bad girl shaped like an hourglass, intelligent, with her own money and great feet."

There's nothing wrong with being specific; the Bible does say, "Ask, and ye shall receive" (John 16:24, KJV). However, the danger comes when we think that if God doesn't bring us a mate who's exactly to our specifications, he's not answering our prayers. What if God is trying to answer your prayers by bringing someone into your life who will fulfill every need, but it just so happens that he or she is very different from your physical ideal? If you're only looking for the ideal, you can miss out.

Of course, finding the right one (or being found by the right one) usually isn't that easy. When you don't meet that person you think is perfect by your self-imposed deadline, it's easy to surrender to panic, discard God's plan, and engage in desperate, reckless behavior in order to make love happen in your life at any cost. This compounds the problem, because everything you see, hear, and read seems to imply that while you're enduring agonizing breakups and awkward first dates, everyone else is finding their happily ever after.

"You're falling behind!" screams your inner narrator. "Where is God?" screams your inner matchmaker. Stressed, envious, and filled with the sense that time is running out, you're desperate to do something—anything—to quell that anxiety. And you're back to the quick fix: date someone you barely know, jump into a stranger's bed, do something foolish and irreversible like rushing into a marriage without God's blessing on it. Inevitably, things fall apart and you're on the side of the road, wounded, surveying the wreckage and wondering what happened.

Let's be clear. Practicing The Wait doesn't mean that you will end up with the One. This is not some genie-in-the-bottle practice that will make your perfect person magically appear. First of all, in God's perfect plan there is one person who is right for each of us who has been called to marriage (an important distinction, because there are some who haven't been called to it). If both people choose to follow God's will, they will find each other. But some don't. Some people veer off and put their will before the Lord's. Does that mean you're meant to be single for the rest of your life?

No, God always has a contingency plan. He's made us compatible with many different types of people. God will provide a way for you to meet someone else who is the right match for the person you are—someone who will bring you joy, happiness, and peace.

As long as you have faith, God will ensure that you will find true happiness with someone who brings out the best in you.

THE WAIT AND . . . WEIGHT

When we started talking about the concept of The Wait and the idea of delaying gratification to get what you want, people were most excited about the idea not as it relates to sex but to weight loss. Nothing, not even sex, stands for instant gratification in our culture more than food. For food, you just have to open the fridge!

Delaying gratification to lose weight makes sense. It's a binary situation: either you eat when you're craving food that isn't good for you or you don't. But if you can delay that need for a quick fix, you can see results over time. Since, according to experts, weight loss is 80 to 90 percent about diet, losing weight really is about controlling what goes in your mouth.

Simple principles can really help: remove temptation (remove from your house those foods that tempt you the most), choose someone you trust to hold and keep you accountable, and work on focusing your attention on the body and health you want more than focusing on the food you can't eat. And pray for strength every step of the way. You'll make it.

THE STAGES OF CELIBACY

The challenges of celibacy change depending on where you are in your dating life. Before we move on, though, let's repeat something that should be obvious but isn't always: *involuntary celibacy isn't The Wait*. You haven't been with anyone in a year because you've hit a dating dry spell? Sorry. Doesn't count. Remember, The Wait is a deliberate choice to delay sexual gratification. If you're stuck in a bad sexual rut, you're probably not thinking about God. You're thinking, "How can I get some sex?" Before you even consider The Wait, get that idea out of your system.

The choice of celibacy comes at one of four stages, each with its own challenges. The first is celibacy while you're dating around. Celibacy is probably most valuable at this stage in your romantic life, because you're clear-headed. You're meeting different people, maybe venturing across racial lines, and you need to keep your wits about you. If you're free of sex, dating is all about getting to know people and yourself.

At this stage, celibacy is easier. You're not overly attached to anybody. You're objective. You're shopping, and while you might try on a pair of shoes in the store, you don't necessarily take them home. To keep your celibacy commitment when you're dating around, remind yourself of what you're doing and of your goals: to meet lots of people, let God work in your spirit, and break problematic patterns.

The second stage is celibacy when you're dating exclusively. You've met one person you really like and you're getting to know them. You're spending a lot of time together and the chemistry is strong. Communication is critical. Early on, you need to let this person know that you're celibate and why. If he or she balks, then that's not the person you are meant to be with. Don't be afraid to walk away and see what else God has in store. If he or she is hip to The Wait, then it's up to you both to keep each other strong and committed. That means avoiding situations that could tempt you and prey on your weakness.

In some ways, this is the most challenging part of celibacy. You really like this person but you're not sure if you're ready to commit to something more serious yet. It's a gray area that's fraught with hazards. One tip: find other ways to feel stimulated when you're together. Find places to have in-depth conversations about things you're curious about. Attend concerts of artists or styles of music you've never experienced before. Set the same fitness goals and work out together. Take a class. Do things that get you excited about each other's mind, creativity, or depth. You'll come away from an evening together feeling fulfilled, knowing that you've stuck to your commitment.

The third stage is, as you might expect, being celibate in a committed relationship. You've decided that yes, this person is worth committing to, and you're ready to be exclusive. This is hopefully the downhill stretch. You can see the finish line—marriage—from where you're standing. That's what helped us be strong during our courtship. Because we got to know each other so well and were completely open about our needs and concerns, marriage wasn't some vague "maybe someday" promise. It was going to happen. We had a time frame. That helped us wait for sex.

There are challenges at this stage, of course. You're spending more time together than ever and talking about a life with each other. Sometimes, you might find yourself thinking, "It's so close, why not just give in? We'll probably get married anyway. In my spirit you're already my spouse." When you're trying to keep your commitment to God at this time, the gift of foresight is incredibly useful. Foresight is the ability to look into the future and imagine the possible (and likely) outcomes to the choices that you make. We're the only beings to whom God has given this gift, and it's a priceless one. It gives us the power to avoid mistakes by being honest with ourselves about might happen if we make choice A versus choice B.

The fourth and final stage comes when you're already in a committed relationship and having sex. Here, you might want to stop and practice The Wait. The fourth and final stage comes when you're already in a committed relationship and having sex. Here, you might want to stop and practice The Wait. Spiritually, this might be because you feel convicted that this is what God wants from you. Practically, you might want to gain more clarity of mind and purpose to see if this person is truly your spouse. No matter the reason, this is probably the hardest of all the stages to practice The Wait because you're already in an established pattern of sexual behavior in your relationship. Having the desire to change this requires courage and conviction.

When you're in The Wait as part of a committed relationship, you're with the person you think God intends you to be with. You can see your potential future laid out in front of you. How will your choices impact that future? If you don't delude yourself and use past relationship decisions as a guide, you can make choices that are more likely to bring you into the fullness of God's best destiny for you. For example, let's say that your pattern is to get into a committed relationship with someone and immediately let sexual desire overwhelm your restraint. This lets you bury obvious problems and pretend that things are fine. However, those problems eventually burst out of the ground like flower bulbs in spring and wreck everything.

Except that this time, you employ your foresight. You

say, "If I let myself go down the same road, I could squander what God's bringing me. So I'm going to keep a level head, be clear, and get to know my partner in every other way." We could see that our relationship had the potential to be incredible—the greatest experience of our lives. That knowledge—and the fear of losing what we could have if we weakened—kept us committed and helped us avoid past traps. You can do the same.

KNOW THAT IT GETS EASIER

One thing we will tell you: living without sex does get easier, especially when you're not in a committed, serious relationship. Initially, it's rough. You're not giving your body what it wants, and like a chocolate lover craving some 70 percent cacao, you're thinking about it all the time. Then some time passes and it gets better. Your mind gains control. Sex can become a pleasurable addiction, and like any addiction it takes time to break free. It will happen. In Gary Keller's book, *The ONE Thing,* he says that it takes sixty-six days to create a new habit. We love applying that idea to The Wait. Sixty-six days of no sex will put you on the path you need to achieve what you want—and what God wants for you. You'll love the clarity, the power, and the feeling of being in control.

WISE WAITING

Celibacy is all about keeping a cool, clear head while you're getting to know someone, and to that end, we suggest that if you drink, go easy on the alcohol during those early dates. We live in a hookup culture, and alcohol is the social lubricant that we use to have fun. But all too often, two people have a few too many drinks and wind up in bed together. That's a great way to find yourself linked to someone you don't even know—and an even better way to end up with a disease or a child.

Monitoring and limiting your drinking, especially during early dates when you're just learning about the person, keeps your head clear and perceptions sharp. It also allows you to present yourself honestly. If you become reckless or the life of the party after a few drinks, you might impair your judgement—something you need if you hope to date successfully.

CHAPTER FOUR

LEAD ME NOT INTO TEMPTATION, I CAN FIND IT MYSELF

Obedience brings peace in decision making. If we have firmly made up our minds to follow the commandments, we will not have to redecide which path to take when temptation comes our way.

—James E. Faust

So you've embraced the idea of The Wait. You've seen the light: getting your head clear and getting your life in order so God can bless you means, first, giving up sex. Good for you. It's a proud move, taking back your power.

Too bad you're miserable, right?

Maybe that's overstating it, but you're thinking about sex a lot, aren't you? Most of your friends are still having it and talking about it. You're trying to be strong, but your body is craving sexual satisfaction. You're used to pursuing sex when you want it, so curtailing the drive to call that "friend with benefits" or hook up with an ex is tough. You know this is the right thing for you, for your life, but . . . man. Temptation is everywhere, and staying strong is brutal.

Believe it, we feel you. We fought the natural desire for more than a year from the time we started dating to the time we married. Some days were better than others, but staying celibate was never easy. We were in love and we were *attracted* to each other. Very, very attracted. Sometimes the sexual chemistry was so hot that we simply couldn't be in the same room together and keep our commitment to celibacy. That's okay; sometimes wisdom means knowing when you're not strong, so that you don't have to be strong. It means seeing that a situation has the potential to pack some serious sexual tension and changing your plans. It means not testing your willpower when you know it's not at its strongest. It means knowing that when you wear *that* dress and he wears *that* suit you can't keep your hands off each other, so you wear something else.

We did all that, but we definitely had moments when it would have been so simple to play the "just this once" game and surrender to what we were feeling. But we didn't. We wanted to remain in control. We wanted to see if we could do what others deemed impossible. We wanted to see if there really was something to be gained by waiting.

We're living, married proof that you can resist temptation and remain celibate even when you're in a committed, marriage-minded relationship with someone you're madly in love with. You can do the same, but not if you don't plan and prepare. You have to accept that temptation is coming for you. Not only that, but unless you live in a monastery, temptation is going to be hanging out pretty much 24-7. You've got to have strategies for dealing with it—for bolstering your will when you're weak, for avoiding the triggers that set off your desire, and for getting the heck out of the room when resistance is futile.

- How will you handle it when dates offer to take you out somewhere that you know might weaken your commitment?
- What will you do when you're close with someone who's clearly ready to get it on with you?
- How can you change your physical environment to manage things that will get you thinking, fantasizing, and obsessing about sex?

Like a Boy or Girl Scout, you've got to be prepared. The Wait isn't for people who think their willpower is so strong

they don't need to think and plan. Nobody's willpower is
bulletproof. If you've already had sex and are used to getting
it, going without it will feel unnatural at first. You can't wing
this. If you're going to make a promise to yourself and God,
do everything in your power to keep it. That means prepar-
ing to deal with and repel temptation, confident that God is
going to hold up His end of the deal. *"No temptation has over-
taken you except what is common to mankind. And God is faithful; he will not let you be tempted beyond what you can bear. But
when you are tempted, he will also provide a way out so that you
can endure it"* (1 Corinthians 10:13, NIV).

REMEMBERING WHY YOU STARTED

If your faith is strong, the hunger to be better and do more
can be reason enough to keep you committed to celibacy. It's
simply not worth it to fail. The possibility that we might miss
out on what God had in store for us was a big part of what
kept us on track.

When you find yourself motivated by a strong desire to
grow into God's purpose, reminding yourself of that goal can
help you remain committed. Here's a prayer that will help
you overcome temptation:

THE LUST PRAYER

God, please help me get control over this beast called Lust. I will not let it destroy me or disrupt the destiny you have set for my life. You said you would provide a way of escape when temptation appears, so show me the exit sign right now, Lord, because I'm about to do something that will please my flesh but harm my spirit. I'm tired of continuously falling prey to lust. I keep falling, getting back up, and falling again. Give me the victory today! I claim authority over my body, my heart, my mind, and my sexuality. You made me sexual but give me the tools to manage this sexuality in a way that pleases you! You said you'd never leave nor forsake me so I'm trusting in you, Lord. You have authority over this lust and I claim that authority now. Be my strength when I am weak and deliver me from this flesh that threatens to destroy every good thing you've planned for my life. I pray this prayer in the mighty name of Jesus, Amen!

THE WAIT AND . . . CREATIVITY

We live in a city and work in an industry where everyone is either trying to act, write or produce a screenplay, become a director, or do something else creative, so we know what frustrated creativity looks like. Everyone has a creative spark; it's part of our legacy from God, the Creator. We're all creators in one way or another. But for those of us dying to find that creative spark and create something great—a script, a play, a poem, a painting, a monologue—finding our creative voice can be torture.

The trouble is that we want to create . . . *now*. Nothing suppresses inspiration like having to be creative on demand. The creative mind isn't Netflix. You can't press a button and order an idea for a movie or a great melody for a song. You have to wait.

The core principles of The Wait apply beautifully to creative people: quieting the mind, listening to the inner voice, letting go of trying to make things happen, doing other things to distract from the need to have results now. When you do that, you free your subconscious, where genius lives. That's when you can create miracles.

WHAT TEMPTATION LOOKS LIKE

But how are you likely to be tempted to break your celibacy pledge? Some scenarios seem obvious: the second-date make-out session that becomes a little too hot and heavy, the beautiful person you just met who invites you to come in after you've had one drink too many. But honestly, how often does that sort of thing really happen? Genuine temptation, we've found, is more insidious. It doesn't seem like you're in trouble until you're more than halfway there. That's when you have to be careful.

For example, what if you're dating someone and he or she dresses for an evening out in something incredibly provocative? Now you've got to spend hours being hot and bothered by how sexy your date looks. You might even start thinking about how good he or she would look out of those clothes. That's a danger zone.

Another one is when you or someone in your circle is in emotional turmoil and just needs "someone to be with." You know how it goes: a fight or breakup, tears, a call asking, "Could you come over for a while?" Now, if you and this other person have no physical attraction to each other, you're probably safe. But if you do, whether you're the crying caller or the one riding to the rescue with ice cream and tissues, watch out. Vulnerable, lonely people just want someone to hold them . . . until that holding turns into something else.

See where we're coming from? Sexual temptation sneaks up on you and catches you when you're weak—which, let's face it, is pretty much whenever you're breathing and awake. Temptation will fit anywhere in your life that you make room for it: work flirtations, having contact with exes, pornography, you name it. In practicing The Wait, one of your goals is to create a lifestyle that acknowledges temptation by putting as many safeguards as possible in place.

That's a lot easier when you can custom fit your anti-temptation plan to your circumstances and triggers. For example, the desire for sex when you're off the dating scene is very different from when you're in a serious relationship.

When you're alone and not dating, opportunities to act on your temptation may not be readily accessible. Maybe you have an office crush or an eye on somebody hot at the gym, but that's about it. Staying strong is really about avoiding stimuli that get you focusing on sex, staying out of provocative situations, and remembering your commitment to God and why you're waiting.

But the serious relationship takes the temptations of dating and ratchets them up. Now you're seeing one person whom you really, really like. You're thinking this could be the person you marry. You're compatible in every way, especially physically. You're spending a lot of private time together. This is torture, right?

No. Remember, the two of us did this, and it did feel like torture at times despite our deep faith and commitment. Besides, even when waiting is hard, at least you're not in it alone anymore. And having a committed partner who will help you do it is a real blessing.

TAKING CARE OF BUSINESS

We're adults, so we're not going to pretend that you haven't been thinking, "But what about masturbation? Can I do that?"

There are many differing opinions about this. Biblically, this is a gray area. The Bible doesn't mention masturbation at all. Ultimately, you'll have to seek God's will for you yourself. However, be careful because masturbation can lead to the development of sin-filled fantasies that can cause the very act to become addictive. In the end, this is a personal issue and should be decided based on personal conviction between you and God. Press into God to figure out what His will is for you regarding this, because for some it's a slippery slope that could become more destructive than helpful.

TEMPTATION AVOIDANCE TIPS

Now we get down to it. What tricks did we use to stay strong and remain celibate even when our bodies were screaming for sexual release? The most powerful tool for staying disciplined and keeping your commitment is your faith in and love of God. If you keep in mind that you're doing this as an act of obedience and to receive the fullness of what God has in store for you, you'll have an easier time avoiding sexual temptation.

It's just as important that you take responsibility for yourself. Some people say, "Well, things just happen." That's a cop-out. We let things happen if we're okay with them, even if we won't admit it to ourselves.

> MEAGAN: When I was nineteen, I struggled with celibacy. But what I really did was abdicate responsibility for my celibacy. I would say, "This man could be my husband, so that would make it OK." Or "Well, I'm not going to initiate sex, so if it happens it's not because *I* made it happen." But I knew that I was putting the responsibility on the other person and not taking ownership of my commitment. It was hypocritical.
>
> Finally, I said, "This is not what the Lord has for me. I'm not going to go into another relationship trying to be celibate and then passively caving on the commitment." I had to make the commitment that sex was absolutely off the table. The crazy thing is that when I did that, God blessed me with somebody who was celibate before I was. It's incredible how things can work out when we're true to God and to ourselves.

MIND YOUR TRIGGERS

Even if your faith has weak moments (which we all have), the most effective way to be successful in your commitment to celibacy is to know your triggers. Avoid setting yourself up for failure. It's not the act of sex that's the problem, but the moments leading up to it. Willpower is wonderful, but at the risk of overdoing the diet metaphor, you don't keep ice cream and chocolate-chip cookies in the house when you're trying to drop fifty pounds. The Lord's Prayer says, "Lead us not into temptation" (Matthew 6:13, KJV), meaning, don't even go there.

Subconsciously, you might put yourself in an environment where sex is a real possibility, believing that if you break your commitment you can shrug and say, "That wasn't my intention, stuff happens." No. You can't stand next to the tracks and then pretend you're not trying to catch a train.

So don't just rely on loving the Lord and being strong. Know yourself. Not to put too fine a point on it, know what makes you horny. Take your triggers out of play, period. If going inside your date's house is likely to lead to serious kissing and possibly other things, say good night at the door. If staying at someone's house after midnight is dangerous for your willpower, agree in advance that everybody will part ways at eleven thirty. If kissing leads down the slippery slope, stop at a hug.

If you're dating someone steadily and you've both agreed to wait, discuss how you're feeling in real time, before you go out. How's your willpower? Is what one of you is wearing pushing the wrong buttons? Is that movie you're planning to see a little too hot? Check in with each other and talk.

Your spirit should be telling your body what to do, not the other way around. That's why you have to keep each other strong. When you get weak, it's your partner's job to say, "No, remember what we're committed to." When your partner weakens, you bring the discipline. Know your limits, monitor yourself, and communicate. If you're feeling particularly susceptible to the temptations of the flesh on a given day, there's nothing wrong with admitting it and communicating about it. Remember, you're both in this together for the long run.

Here are some major triggers to be mindful of:

- *Late nights.* Movie night on the couch in somebody's apartment is fun, but it can lead to more.
- *Emotional trauma.* When you get in a fight with someone, get in trouble at work, or just feel bad, you're vulnerable and want comfort. Be careful.
- *Intimate contact.* Be affectionate, but be mindful if that affection is making it difficult for you or the person you're dating to resist temptation. If it is, dial down the intensity.
- *Alcohol.* Drinking and celibacy probably isn't the best mix. Liquor reduces your inhibitions and makes you more likely to do something you'll regret. If you're waiting, consider doing it sober. Either that or make

the choice not to drink (or drink minimally) around
the person you're dating.

• *Sexting and Snapchat*. Provocative texts or video clips can
send you over the edge if your willpower is wavering.

• *Travel*. Hookups on the road can seem like they don't
count, kind of like calories from ice cream that you eat
when nobody's watching. What? Of course sex when
you're on the road counts. Don't fool yourself.

PREPARE FOR EVERY CONTINGENCY

Anything that helps you stay disciplined is fair game. Use
whatever works to keep you waiting and fulfilling your commitment. Because while few things are harder to wait on
than sex, nothing else will bring you more blessings. Some
suggestions:

Put technology to work for you. If needed, set a "go home"
alarm on your smartphone. Ask a friend to send you an "Are
you guys being good?" text message at a preset time.

Avoid people who talk about sex all the time. They don't
have to be jerks trying to sabotage you. Some people just
can't help talking about sex; it's their favorite subject. They
talk about their own sexual exploits, sex in TV and film, and
so on. This might be the guy who looks at a girl in a club

and says, "Oooh, look at that. Mmmm, I know what I'd do to her," and then tells you in detail. Apart from being crass, that's narration you might not need. Know how you're feeling, and if you're feeling weak, ask such people to change the conversation.

Double-date or date in social groups. Going out with a group is fun and it reduces the pressure that sometimes comes with going out on a one-on-one date. Choose people who are supportive of your decision to be celibate and who respect your goals.

Control your environment. Some places are inherently charged with sexual energy: nightclubs, strip clubs, and the like. Sometimes, it's not the location but the situation, like a late-night work session with an attractive colleague or a study session with a cute friend. If you want to avoid temptation, avoid environments and situations that breed it. Take dates to places that are fun but not sensual. Avoid intimate solo time with people to whom you're attracted, whether they're from work, church, or school. This doesn't make you weak and it doesn't make you a chicken. It makes you smart.

Try to stay away from graphic sexual imagery. If you don't want to drive the car, why on earth would you start the engine? It's incredibly easy to find graphic sexuality in our culture, especially online, and it's become a daily habit for some. Break it. Clear your browser cache and delete any bookmarks you have to websites that show suggestive images. We're not trying to be prudish here, but let's be honest. We've got to be active in managing this area of life. Some of this stuff is graphic and incredibly hot. Watching or seeing others having sex is usually going to make you want to have it, too. Manage the temptation by removing sexual images from your life.

Stay busy. Remember, an idle mind is the devil's playground. Find activities you enjoy doing that allow you to channel and use your energy in positive, constructive, life-improving ways. Put in more hours at work (go for that promotion). Volunteer. Travel. Work on your house. Join a ministry at the church. Teach classes or mentor someone. Fill up your days so your focus is on what you're doing, not what you're not doing.

You can do this. We know, because we did it.

EYES ON THE PRIZE

Celibacy can have a certain allure when you're with someone you think you want to spend your life with: *If we can wait to have sex until after marriage, the sex is going to be absolutely mind-blowing*. That may or may not be true. Every couple is different. It takes a while to get to know your spouse sexually, so while the wedding night is great, don't set expectations so high that you set yourself up for disappointment.

If you commit to getting to know your spouse sexually, you will have incredible sex (in due time). However, sex shouldn't just be about physical gratification, but sensual excitement and spiritual connection as well—the tease, the hint, the mystery of what's hidden. In the interim, while you wait, remember that true sexuality is about confidence, intelligence, and connection. Cultivate those things in your relationship and the sex will be beyond compare.

But there's an even deeper level to consider. When you're feeling weak, remember why you're forgoing sex in the first place. You want to receive God's best in all areas of your life, the true destiny He has planned for you. You want the full course of wonder and joy in your life: career, purpose, love, excitement . . . you name it. That's why you're waiting. Why would you mess that up for a few minutes of pleasure?

THINKING ABOUT SEX LESS

Hamlet said, "There is nothing either good or bad, but thinking makes it so." When the subject is sex, truer words were never spoken. When we can't have something, we can't stop thinking about it. When that something is sex, the endless thought makes it harder to stay committed and tempts us to chase empty gratification. The solution: stop thinking about sex so much. Yes, we know that's like an elephant sitting in the middle of a room while someone's telling you, "Don't think about the elephant!" But it can be done.

- Pray or meditate every day, multiple times a day. Both will help quiet anxiety and promote calm.
- If you know others who are practicing The Wait or who are celibate for other reasons, create a support group, even if it's a virtual one on a site such as Google+.
- Carry a meaningful object or token that reminds you of your commitment to God and to celibacy.
- Write down a statement of why you're choosing to wait and keep it in your phone. Reminding yourself of why you're doing it is key to keeping the commitment.
- Ask friends who keep sending you sexual material to stop.

Is it over the top to avoid friends who talk about sex, music that promotes it, or movies with love-making scenes? It all depends on your triggers. Things that get one person obsessing about sex will have zero effect on another person. Figure out what gets you dwelling on those things that fuel your lust and take steps to avoid it. Remember, commitment is half willpower and half common sense.

CHAPTER FIVE

WHAT KEEPS WOMEN FROM WAITING?

Don't be afraid to lose him, because if a man
truly loves you, he's not going anywhere.
—STEVE HARVEY, *ACT LIKE A LADY, THINK LIKE A MAN*

There's a scene in the classic movie *When Harry Met Sally* that perfectly captures the subject of this chapter. In it, Sally, the main character played by Meg Ryan, is hesitating to get back into the dating pool after a bad breakup. Her friends Marie and Alice issue an ominous warning:

Marie: Okay. But don't wait too long. Remember what happened with David Warsaw? His wife left him, and everyone said, give him some time, don't move in too fast. *Six months later, he was dead.*

Sally: What are you saying? I should get married to someone right away in case he's about to die?

Alice: At least you can say you were married.

Is it us, or is that concept completely crazy? Getting married just for the sake of being married belongs in the Bad Decision Hall of Fame. But even though society has changed, and more and more millennial women are choosing not to get married, the white dress still has the power to enchant. In a 2012 survey of more than 2,500 female college students done by Her Campus Media, 85 percent said that they wanted to be married by the time they turned thirty.

This is one of the ways in which men and women are very different, and that's why we've written these two chapters. When it comes to the reasons people wait for sex or don't, women and men could not be more different. Men might not be as marriage-phobic as the pop culture stereotypes suggest, but they're still not lining up to get married or having anxiety attacks if nobody's "put a ring on it" by the time they blow past thirty. In fact, a lot of guys are just getting started with their lives at thirty.

All the while, more than a few single women the same age are expressing anxiety to their girlfriends about their biological clocks, worrying about becoming older and lonely, and starting to wonder what's wrong with them if nobody has popped the question. Many women seem to be obsessed with somebody—anybody—telling them that they are loved and cared for, even if that turns out to be a lie.

Author and blogger Tracy McMillan absolutely nails it in an article that appeared on the *Huffington Post* called "Why You're Not Married":

> Hooking up with some guy in a hot tub on a rooftop is fine for some of the ladies of *Jersey Shore*—but they're not trying to get married. You are. Which means, unfortunately, that if you're having sex outside committed relationships, you will have to stop. Why? Because past a certain age, casual sex is like recreational heroin—it doesn't stay recreational for long.
>
> That's due in part to this thing called oxytocin—a bonding hormone that is released when a woman a) nurses her baby and b) has an orgasm—that will totally mess up your casual-sex game. It's why you can be [hooking up] with some dude who isn't even all that great and the next thing you know, *you're totally strung out on him.* And you have no idea how it happened. Oxytocin, that's how it happened. And since nature can't discriminate between marriage material and Charlie Sheen, you're going to have to start being way more selective than you are right now.

Now that's keeping it really real! And she's right. What's going on here? Besides the power of hormones, the force that typically drives women into the arms of guy after guy, even if most of those so-called relationships end in screaming matches or devastating infidelity, is fear. Scratch the surface of a lot of unmarried young women and you'll find a layer of fear just below the surface. Fear of being alone. Fear of not having children. Fear of being judged and found wanting. Fear of being less of a woman. Fear of being inadequate, insufficient, not good enough. Fear of not being all you were called to be by the time you think it should happen.

HAPPILY EVER AFTER? NOT SO MUCH

The two of us work in the entertainment industry, so we're cogs in the machine that's partially responsible for the state of confusion so many women are in. Movies and television are steeped in the mythology that a woman is only as good as the man she captures, and what captures that man is sex. Messed up as that is, it's become a cultural touchstone that's shaped everything about what young women believe they're supposed to have and supposed to want. For example:

- Quick, other than *Frozen*, name a Disney animated feature with a female protagonist that doesn't end with her either getting married or catching a guy (usually a prince) who will obviously become her husband. From *Snow White* and *Sleeping Beauty* to *Tangled* and *The Princess and the Frog*, we'll bet you can't do it. That's three generations of impressionable young girls who've grown up believing that their highest, best purpose was to marry a prince and . . . then what? What happens after happily ever after?

- Movies we label "chick flicks" are usually romantic comedies, right? By definition, those almost always end with one or more couples pairing off and sometimes walking down the aisle. Take your pick, from *My Best Friend's Wedding* to *Love, Actually* and even to *Jumping the Broom*. They're all about the female fantasy of finding and falling in love with the perfect man. Could you see the typical "guy movie" ending the same way, with Vin Diesel or the Rock walking down the aisle with their leading lady while stuff explodes in the background? Neither could we.

- Do you remember the "you complete me" line from *Jerry Maguire?* True, Tom Cruise's character says the line in the movie, but the idea—that we need a soul mate to complete us and make us whole—is troubling. Because the reality most women face is very different.

When God created you, He made you a whole woman. He did the same for every woman. Each woman is complete unto herself, a child of the Lord with everything she needs to grow into a source of love, light, and power in this world. If that's true, then why do most women believe the truest form of happiness can only be achieved once they find Mr. Right?

It's because while God created you as a complete being unto yourself, He also created man to be your partner, the one who brings out the very best of you. That's not the same as needing a man to complete you. God intends for us to bring out the best versions of each other. Your husband is your partner in purpose. He's the person God put on your team, and the two of you are supposed to hold each other accountable, hold up a mirror to each other, be each other's cheerleader, and help each other accomplish your individual and collective purposes.

The thing is, you can't just go out and find that man. He also has to find you, and that won't happen until you're ready. So you should work on becoming a whole, fully realized woman before you even think about committing to being any man's wife. You don't necessarily need a man to be your best self; it's quite possible that God will allow you to achieve your full potential and fulfill your part in His plan without a man in your life first. If a man does come into your life, he ought to inspire you to achieve even greater fulfillment. A woman might live her entire life without a man and be completely fulfilled, empowered, and complete. We've known a few who have.

As a woman, it's your responsibility to work on developing the fullness of who God created you to be before you give yourself to your husband. Until you do that, you won't be ready to find and keep that perfect partner. God, not man, completes you.

WOMEN'S DISCIPLINES

Like working out or eating low-carb, The Wait is a discipline. It's difficult to sustain a life without sex, possibly because it's counter to the way you've conducted your life up to now. That means it's important to have a set of disciplined practices that will keep you focused, positive, and gaining new strength over time. For women, these might include:

- Regular prayer (a must)
- Meditating: making time to have self-reflection on areas of growth or needed growth
- Fasting
- Self-care, such as getting enough sleep
- Doing something positive to increase your self-confidence
- Journaling
- Talking with a pastor or spiritual mentor
- Getting counsel from other women who have successfully waited
- Growing your career
- Examining past relationship patterns
- Making peace with people from your past who hurt you or with whom you have unresolved conflict

FOR WOMEN, CELIBACY IS CONTROL

The trouble is, many women can't accept that they can be complete without a man. Despite all the incredible gains that women have made in our society—running huge corporations, filling high positions in government, possibly being the next president of the United States—we still live in an era that defines women largely according to their sexuality and appearance.

One way this stereotype plays out is in the idea that a woman can't be the pursuer in a relationship. The man is supposed to initiate the action, make the first move, offer to pay for dinner, and so on. Hunter and prey, right? Is this how it's supposed to be?

There are as many different women's natures as there are women. There are plenty of women who take the initiative. They extend the first invitation or they don't call a guy until they're good and ready. The cliché of the desperate woman waiting by the phone for last night's date to call is so 1990, and not just because nobody has a landline anymore. The difference is that while a woman today might date more like a man, she'll often bring a female sensibility to it. And a healthy woman will protect her heart by waiting until she has a clear emotional connection with a guy before getting too serious with him.

Smart women know that sex is power, and waiting is the ultimate act of claiming that power. Celibacy is control. Since most men date in the hopes of having sex at the end of the date, you're the one calling the shots. Of course, there's a fine line. It's possible to use sex as a weapon or a tool—something that should be avoided.

MEAGAN: As a teenager and Christian, I was taught to wait. Because of this, I was the last of my friends to lose her virginity. But that idea shaped not only my identity as a woman but also the way I saw men.

I grew up in Canyon Country, north of Los Angeles. My father was not in the home. My parents had separated and ultimately my dad moved on with someone else. My father is and always has been an incredible man, but as a child watching my mother's devastation taught me to treat relationships like they would always end. The message was "Never trust a man. Never allow yourself to be in a position to fall apart." I approached every relationship with the attitude that as women, we always get the shorter end of the stick. A man can give us something—literally put something inside us—and we are on the physical and emotional end of however that works out. So in my twenties, I always treated serious relationships as 40/60. I gave only 40 percent so I could protect myself. I always needed to be 100 percent ready to pick up the pieces and be unaffected if and when things didn't work out.

During this time, I discovered my essential nature as a woman: I found that I needed emotional connection less than most girls, but I think that may have been because I conditioned myself to need it less. I didn't find myself at home crying because someone didn't call me, because I would cut him off first. I would hurt him before he could hurt me.

I was avoiding failure and heartbreak. But I was also preventing myself from experiencing any real emotional or spiritual growth, because I wasn't letting any guy of substance get close enough to challenge the way I acted or thought. That wasn't a healthy way to date. If a guy challenged me when the relationship was in the early stages, I would try to be accommodating and submit to a degree. However, when the relationship got past the early stages, any proposed changes that I didn't agree with made me resentful. This would ultimately lead to the relationship's demise.

Those were the years that I thought I was very much in control . . . more in control than I actually was.

It's a tightrope many women have to walk: have sex and be called a slut, or withhold sex and get labeled a prude or a tease. It's a no-win situation . . . unless you're clear about why you're handling your sexual and dating life as you are. If you're practicing The Wait, abstaining from sex is something you're doing for yourself, not as a sort of brake you apply to your relationship. Forgoing sexual intercourse so you can become a more self-aware, completely realized woman is an empowering choice, one worth making.

"IF I DON'T SLEEP WITH HIM, I'LL LOSE HIM"

Some women who would love to be celibate just can't do it because they're afraid they'll lose their man if they don't sleep with him.

Let's be honest: there are some men who won't go along with a woman's vow to abstain until marriage. They simply won't consider it. However, this isn't something you should fear. While choosing celibacy isn't easy for either a man or a woman, the right man will be open to waiting for the woman he loves and knows he is destined to be with.

Here's a secret about men, ladies:

A man who says no to celibacy isn't making
a statement about you. It's about him.

Men's identity is closely tied to their sexuality. Many a man faced with a celibate relationship is going to worry that other men will make fun of him and think him less of a man because he's not getting any. He's going to say no to you because he's used to women who will offer sex as a way to keep him happy. He's going to consider every way to keep getting what he wants—to keep feeling manly and looking manly to his manly friends—even if that means he must get that from another woman.

If you're compatible and really care about each other and he still bolts as soon as you suggest The Wait, he's really saying, "I'm not strong or evolved enough to go without sex." An admission like this might also reveal that he doesn't see a long-term future with you—a good thing to know sooner rather than later so you don't waste more of your time.

No woman should fear finding out that the guy she's seeing won't consider celibacy. A man leaving over sex is a blessing, because it tells you that he wasn't your husband. On the other hand, if you ditch celibacy out of desperation to keep him, you could end up wasting years with the wrong person. Worse yet, you might marry a man whose lack of sexual discipline lays the foundation for infidelity down the line.

HOW NOT TO WAIT

You're going to catch a ton of grief from some of the people in your life anytime you decide to go against the norm. That's par for the course. But there's no reason to let other people's lack of understanding derail your Wait, especially early on when it would be *so* easy to say, "Okay, just one night isn't going to hurt anything."

If you're a woman new to The Wait, there are definitely some things you might want to avoid:

- Communication from drama-prone girlfriends. Sisters-in-arms can turn toxic if they think you're making the choice they should be making but can't. Or maybe your mom is pressuring you about marriage or motherhood. She'll fret, lecture, and try to get you back in the pool. Spare yourself (and preserve your friendship) and steer clear of them for a bit.

- Exes. Do we really have to explain why this is a bad idea? If you're trying to build a new, healthy life, the last thing you need is someone who has the potential to take you back into the very bad habits you're trying to break.

"THERE ARE ONLY A FEW GOOD MEN OUT THERE"

Another obstacle that makes it hard for women to wait is the idea that they're all in competition with one another for a limited supply of decent men. That's toxic to self-esteem and spiritual growth. We serve a God who has an infinite number of ways to bless a woman with the right person. Yet if we believe there are only "a few," that's when the trouble starts.

This notion of scarcity prompts women to fight it out for what they see as a dwindling supply of good, quality guys who are willing to commit to marriage. It propagates a host of dangerous stereotypes:

- Most of the men out there are worthless players who want nothing to do with marriage or commitment.
- The few good men who do want to get married know they have their pick of the pool, so women have to do anything and everything to catch one before he gets away.

In fact, none of this is true. Excluding racial dating preferences, statistician Jonathan Soma recently put together a map that shows the ratio of single women to single men around the country, and amazingly, in the twenty-to-twenty-nine age group there are more single men than single women in almost every major city. But facts have little power over fears. Fear that they could chase "the man who got away" puts women under tremendous pressure to compromise their morality and to live according to what the men in their circles want even if it contradicts what God wants.

Also, according to a recent Pew Research Center study of marriage, a number of key findings debunk many of the stereotypes about men not being interested in marriage:

- Most Americans do marry—about nine in ten adults over forty-five have been married at least once.
- Among married people surveyed, 93 percent say that love is a very important reason to get married; 84 percent of unmarried people say so. Men and women are equally likely to say love is a very important reason to get married.
- Men are just as likely as women to say they want to marry.
- Men believe in true love.

Even Match.com's most recent Singles in America report paints a very different picture of men and love. Match.com surveyed more than 5,600 singles across the nation, of every ethnicity, from ages seventeen to seventy, about their attitudes and behaviors toward relationships, and this is some of what they found:

- 87 percent of men would date a woman who makes more money than they do.
- 90 percent of men are okay with a woman asking them out.
- 87 percent of men would date a woman who's more educated than they are.
- 90 percent of men consider having a sense of humor just as important as physical attractiveness.
- 89 percent of all men and women believe you can stay married to the same person forever.

Based on this information, perhaps men aren't quite as hopeless about commitment and relationships as we've been led to believe. In other words, there's hope.

WOMAN VERSUS WOMAN

Actually, it's when women get into competition with each other for men that things can get hurtful. The woman-versus-woman conflict can produce serious collateral damage. First, it makes relationships between women tense, envious, and often ugly. Instead of sisters linking arms to try and make things better for each other, they can become like boxers in heels, feinting and jabbing, looking for an opening so they can knock out any woman who might be untrustworthy competition. What else?

- *Drama.* Lots of drama. The drama of competition and the desperation it breeds causes long-term emotional damage. We've seen this type of drama over a man rip families apart to the point that certain women don't even speak to each other anymore.
- *Depression.* Women are more prone to depression than men, and feelings of worthlessness over failed relationships can contribute to this.
- *Loss of identity.* When a woman believes she has to compete with another woman for a man, that woman can become consumed with thinking about how to get or keep the man. The odds are the woman will become whatever the man wants in order to keep him, even if it costs her true identity. That's a time bomb, because no one can live like that forever. Eventually she'll resent him for making her be someone she's not, and the relationship will explode.

The great irony of all this is that women really aren't competing with other women. You're only competing with yourself. When you practice The Wait and make the powerful choice to be celibate and be in control, other women don't matter. Neither do men, for that matter. God has a unique, specific plan for all of our lives.

The Wait is about you winning the battle over that unaffirmed, lonely, needy, or desperate feeling inside and refusing to let it drive your choices or determine your actions. It's about becoming complete in yourself so that the real gifts that you bring to a relationship go far beyond sexuality. It's about knowing what you want from a man, being confident and at peace that God will send that man, and believing it won't require a compromise of the flesh to keep him.

WHO IS YOUR HUSBAND?

That man whose maturity, depth, and patience equal your own is your husband. But before we get into what a husband really is, let's be clear: the husband God has for you is not necessarily the man you decide to marry, especially if you marry him out of panic, desperation, fear, or envy that your BFF got hitched before you did. Such a man is merely *a* husband.

God's definition of *your* husband is that man who helps you become the best version of yourself and wants you to help him do the same. He's the man who values and respects you for your ownership of yourself. This man will also respect you in your restraint in practicing The Wait. He's the man who won't run away when you tell him you're abstaining from sex because he understands and appreciates the reasons why you're doing it. He might already be on the same path himself. Your husband is the person you were meant to be with, put into your path by God. He's your partner in purpose.

This definition of a husband counters all the disempowering, negative stereotypes. Your husband is the man whose strengths complement your own, who brings out the best of your talents, wisdom, intelligence, and compassion. He's the man who will not diminish you to lift himself up, but rather takes joy and pride in your accomplishments, even if they exceed his own. He's the fully realized man God has meant you to be with.

Committing to your husband doesn't mean surrendering yourself. When you're able to recognize your husband for who he is you'll have begun the process of becoming a different person—based on your own values and wisdom, but also based on your obedience to God's timetable. You'll be ready.

MEAGAN: When you fall into relationships but then abandon them fast, you don't get away clean. You give pieces of yourself away and don't realize it until you're down the road.

Choices I thought I was making out of strength were

actually out of weakness and fear. I thought I was being strong because I controlled each situation, but my version of control was about not getting hurt, not about learning to know myself or the guy I was with. Later, when I decided to approach things fearlessly, more wholeheartedly, I ended up walking into an emotionally and sometimes verbally abusive relationship. I'd had enough.

I decided to slow down and commit to being celibate. More important, I was called to see that I was in a different space in my life. None of what I had done in my twenties had worked. God had let me learn and make my mistakes, but now it was time for me to do it God's way, truly. You see, I had given him most of my life but left this one challenging area to chance.

It was time for me to grow spiritually, get closer to and go deeper into God, and let him put the pieces of my life back together. Life became about not getting sidetracked or allowing confusion to send me spinning back to my old ways. As God worked, I started to get clarity that things were coming together.

To my amazement, during this time, God told me in my spirit that DeVon was my husband. I was still in that crazy, self-destructive space and I said, "Okay, what do I do with this?" God said, "Just wait. You need to work through the things you are working through." The Wait was first about my time with God, the time I needed to begin the healing process and grow.

Those nine months between God telling me that DeVon was my husband and DeVon asking me out on our first date was one of the toughest times of my life . . . and one of the most rewarding. I was casting off old parts of myself that weren't working for me anymore and discovering who I truly was.

Marriage brings self-awareness, transformation, growth, healing, and change, but partnering with your husband is designed to bring out the best in you. Your husband will challenge you in new ways, see things you might have missed, and believe in you when no one else does (sometimes even you).

Don't worry, there's plenty of room for romance, excitement, and being madly in love in this kind of relationship. But it's a deeper, richer love built on maturity, respect, and faith. With your husband, you'll be just as giddy as you were with every new guy when you were dating around. But you'll also know that this is real. Even better, it's blessed, because you've come together as an express part of God's will. You were meant to be with each other, and that's a kind of joy that few couples experience.

So the question is, do you want *a* husband or *your* husband? *A* husband is a human Band-Aid who temporarily covers a wound that he can't ever heal. *Your* husband can be used by God to bring real, lasting healing. He is the man who's worthy of you as you become who you are meant to be. He might be in your life long before you're ready but you won't recognize each other if you're still operating from a place of incompleteness. Your husband won't become apparent to you until you've begun to rid yourself of your old habits and patterns, gone through a time of prayer and growth, and reached that point where you recognize your own wholeness. You might want a man in your life, but you don't need one. You understand that God made you complete; you are sufficient. That's when it's time for God to bring your husband into your awareness.

FEAR IS A FAILURE OF FAITH

It takes courage and faith to wait for your husband in this way. Because the greatest fear of all is the fear that God will not keep His promises. He won't come through for you.

But God doesn't fail to deliver; we fail to believe we are worthy. It takes faith to accept that the right man will come, even if there are obstacles in the way. It takes guts to face your fears and say, "I have faith that God is going to bring me the right person, so I'm going to wait until He does." If you can find the courage to let a man walk away, you can find the courage to wait.

> MEAGAN: I'll never forget this conversation: I was talking to a friend and saying that if a certain hot guy didn't approach me I'd walk away. I was fine just letting him go. My friend got terribly offended and said, "Not every girl can do that. Not every girl can just stand there and let the guy walk away if he doesn't approach her."
>
> There's a belief among some women that if they aren't proactive they won't end up with anyone. The question is, why do you want to be with someone? If your reason is, "Another man might not come along," you're in a bad place. You're acting purely out of fear, and that means you don't trust God.

This is true for so many things in life. When you frantically chase after something, like a dog chasing a car, it actually becomes harder and harder for you to catch. You start making compromises and forgetting who you are, and before long you've become someone else. You've lost the very qualities that made it possible for you to catch what you were chasing. That's true for love, career, wealth, you name it.

But when you focus on doing the right things and becoming a person to whom good things happen, good things do happen. The apostle Paul said it best: "So let's not allow ourselves to get fatigued doing good. At the right time we will harvest a good crop if we don't give up, or quit. Right now, therefore, every time we get the chance, let us work for the benefit of all, starting with the people closest to us in the community of faith" (Galatians 6:9–10, MSG).

The process of finding your husband isn't really about finding your husband but about finding yourself as a woman. One vital thing to remember, though:

> *Who you think you should end up with*
> *is rarely who you do end up with.*

That was certainly true for us. It makes sense. If you're engaged in a process of change and self-discovery, you're becoming a different woman each day. There's no telling what kind of man will be your perfect partner when the process is complete. You have to be open and on the lookout for people God might be putting in your path. One of the components to this is to be open to love in whatever package God wants to bring it to you. What if your God-ordained husband comes in a package you aren't expecting, such as a different race, a shorter stature, or a look that differs from your physical ideal? Will you give him a chance or reject him?

THE WAIT AND . . . FRIENDSHIPS

In their own way, friendships between women are much more complicated than romantic relationships. When a man and a woman date, marriage can be the goal. With friends, it's not always clear what you are to each other. Rivals? Sisters? Foils? Each other's biggest fans?

Sometimes, when women are in the same stage of life, worrying about men and marriage and children and all the rest, things get tense. It's tempting to turn your back on something that's so much trouble. But what if you waited? What if you let the friendship find a natural rhythm for this changing time in your lives? After all, if you're changing, why would your friendship stay the same?

Patience, forbearance, kindness, understanding, and frank communication go a long way to easing tension between women. Practice that aspect of The Wait with each other.

Ask questions and share honestly. You might be reunited with friends you thought you'd lost.

WAITING GIVES YOU BACK YOUR POWER

The most potent aspect of The Wait for women goes back to power. Practicing The Wait gives you back your power—but not at someone else's expense. You're not withholding sex to punish or manipulate a man. You're not cutting down a boyfriend to embarrass him or to balance your insecurities. You're not doing the "I'm going to dump you before you dump me" routine. You don't need to play those games to hold your power, because you're choosing not to be manipulated, not to let social or cultural expectations pull your strings.

MEAGAN: Waiting is an act of power. It's declaring that you know and accept yourself, love yourself, and trust God. Growing up, I was skinny, awkward, short, and had a huge gap in my teeth. I had big, curly Afro hair. The boys I liked never liked me back; I remember one boy who said he didn't like me because I didn't have boobs, which was hurtful. I thought, "Well, they just don't see how great I am yet."

As a result, I spent years feeling I needed validation from my peers. Until you reach a point where don't need that, you can't wait. But once you find that place where you can say, "I don't need anyone else to tell me my worth," you can.

The true power and beauty of The Wait is bigger than finding a husband who supports, protects, and champions you or is your partner in purpose. It's that you really get to enjoy being the woman God created you to be. You don't have to carry the stress of wondering if the man you're with really supports you. You get to be the backbone. You get to hone in on all the things that make being a woman special and empowering. If you don't take strength into the relationship, what's the point? With DeVon, I get to be a real and powerful woman instead of some idealized version.

God has a destiny set up for you, but you get to choose whether or not to follow it. That's power. That's free will. You decide how to express God's vision for who you will be. And just as your husband will, God wants you to be powerful and confident and self-aware. That's the best version of you.

Some people think that women are inferior to men. But you're not. Both sexes are equal. The first woman came from a man, and every man since has come from a woman. The Wait helps you get clear on this—helps you understand your strengths, take pride in your position, and love yourself.

HOW WAITING GETS YOU WHAT YOU WANT

Practicing The Wait changes you into a woman who will attract, recognize, and connect with your destiny on every level. It aligns you with God's perfect will for your life, and the benefits of this alignment will improve every area of your life dramatically. When you consciously take time to observe, pray, reflect, practice self-care, work on your career, commit to wholeness, and choose God's will over yours, you will begin to see amazing things happen that will bring you joy and peace you thought was impossible.

At first The Wait might seem uncomfortable, even lonely. But as you progress, your comfort grows. You start to see yourself not in the context of dating, sex, men, or other women, but as you. After a while, you actually start to see yourself as God sees you: a powerful source of love and life and healing and so much more. You can be abstinent and control your sexuality. You can have a thriving career and a happy personal life. You can be brilliant, gorgeous, and assertive without having to apologize for it. You do deserve the life that God's had waiting for you all this time.

When you wait, things become clear. It's a bit like walking out of an amusement park into the real world: the rides and games and colorful distractions are gone and things seem a little dull, but then you realize that everything's open to you from horizon to horizon. That's empowering. Just as empowering is stepping back, clearing your head, and asking the kind of perception-sharpening questions you realize you should have been asking all along:

- What have I been spending my energy and attention on and why?
- What have I been compromising to do that?
- Is what I'm doing filling me up or emptying me out?
- What is the driving force in my choices?
- What am I ready to sacrifice in order to change things and become my best self?

They're not easy questions to answer, especially if doing so means confronting the fact that you've been hiding sick self-esteem or lifelong wounds underneath the disguise of a flirty serial dater. But if you have the courage to face the answers (and you do), they'll tell you something profound: living fully is not about needing a man to complete you. It's about wanting a man to partner with, to walk alongside the incredible woman you're on the way to becoming . . . to be the woman you were destined to be.

That last question, about sacrifice, can be challenging. In the book of Romans, the apostle Paul says, "Therefore, I urge you, brothers and sisters, in view of God's mercy, to offer your bodies as a living sacrifice, holy and pleasing to God—this is your true and proper worship. Do not conform to the pattern of this world, but be transformed by the renewing of your mind. Then you will be able to test and approve what God's will is—his good, pleasing and perfect will" (Romans

12:1–2, NIV). Make no mistake: you're going to have to give something up to wait. You must let go of the old, fearful, doubting version of yourself so the new, brave, fearless woman inside you can emerge.

For women, the reward of The Wait is not about the desire to find your husband but the reward of peace, knowing you are living in the seat of God's will for your life. Do that and you leave him no choice but to bless you with His very best.

CHAPTER SIX

WHAT KEEPS MEN FROM WAITING?

Women need a reason to have sex. Men just need a place.
—BILLY CRYSTAL, *CITY SLICKERS*

A man who is a master of patience
is master of everything else.
—GEORGE SAVILE

Now, from the subtlety and questioning sincerity of women, we take you to . . . men. Not exactly a group of people associated with an eagerness to go without sex. But make no mistake, men suffer just as much as women do from the expectations and delusions surrounding sexuality and romance. In fact, men's common inability to wait betrays a deep insecurity next to which women's fears pale in comparison.

See, deliberately not having sex is a totally foreign concept to most guys. It's no accident that we often talk about a

boy "becoming a man" when he has his first sexual experience. At the same time, while many women may seem eager,
even desperate, to lock up some sort of commitment, many
men run screaming into the night at the mere mention of the
word.

Hook up with no strings attached? All right, cool, let's get it on.

*Put a ring on it? Oh, look at the time, that's work calling, I'll
text you, babe, I got to go.*

Guys are eternally cavalier about this sex-first, commitment-
never values system. Talk to a group of men in a club or out
on the basketball court about their conquests, and before long
the whole thing turns into a gathering of fourteen-year-olds
in a locker room: a festival of laughing high fives and who's-
had-more comparisons. But this isn't a laughing matter. Just as
some women do real damage by throwing themselves at every
potential husband, men inflict genuine self-harm by burning
endless time, energy, and money in pursuit of meaningless self-
gratification.

It's a waste, and it's not necessary. We're not ready to say
"boys will be boys" and dismiss men as overgrown adolescents doomed to follow their genitalia over the cliff to humil-
iation, financial ruin, and even prison. God gave men their
sex drive, but He also gifted them with restraint, passion,
wisdom, a restless and bold creativity, and the ability to lead
and inspire. If you're a man, all those qualities are in you.

All you need is to stop doing the things that keep God's gifts from being fully expressed in you.

That means learning to practice The Wait. But before we talk about how, let's take a closer look at why men hate to wait.

DEVON: The decision to wait was probably one of the most difficult ones I've ever made in my life. I was young, had a high-profile executive job in Hollywood, was making good money and driving a nice car—for all intents and purposes I was living the life most men aspire to live, yet I wasn't having sex. There were many times when I questioned my own stance—not because I didn't believe in it but because it was lonely. No one I knew, Christian or otherwise, was maintaining the commitment for as long as I was. There were many nights I even questioned my own manhood, thinking, "Am I a real man without sex? Am I living an abnormal, unnatural life?"

I was publicly and privately ridiculed at times by some who knew of my commitment, even to the point of people questioning my sexual orientation. It hurt me deeply. These were the challenges I had to battle. Yet, even at my weakest, there was this voice in my head that kept saying, "Keep going." Even when there was no end in sight, even when I couldn't turn to anyone but God to give me direction and strength, I knew that buried inside the commitment were the keys to an amazing life. I can tell you now I was right to have faith. The incredible personal and professional success I have is directly related to my decision to wait.

THE LIST

In her book *The Eclipse: A Memoir of Suicide,* Antonella Gambotto-Burke writes,

> *The self-esteem of western women is founded on physical being (body mass index, youth, beauty). This creates a tricky emphasis on image, but the internalized locus of self-worth saves lives. Western men are very different. In externalizing the source of their self-esteem, they surrender all emotional independence. (Conquest requires two parties, after all.) A man cannot feel like a man without a partner, corporation, team. Manhood is a game played on the terrain of opposites. It thus follows that male sense of self disintegrates when the Other is absent.*

That observation reflects a profound difference between the sexes' ability to practice The Wait. Women, however they might stumble and fall in their commitment to celibacy, are mostly trying to satisfy themselves, not impress other women.

Men are exactly the opposite. Habitual players who drive flashy cars and keep a database of women on call do so to curry favor with their boys. Being known as a "pimp" and dating multiple ladies while keeping it cool and dodging drama is the ultimate demonstration of having game. Approval, validation, and self-worth are all based on what other guys think.

Trouble is, if you're the man in your circle and you decide to step up and challenge the male status quo, you will be met with resistance from other men who want you to think that waiting makes men less masculine. The thinking goes like this: The more conquests you have, the more validation you get from others, and the more validation you get, the better you feel. The more notches on your belt, the more you look like a player, and the more women want you. And so on, round and round. With this ethos permeating every part of male culture, the practice of celibacy isn't just inconceivable. It's perceived as insane.

The List is that unspoken inventory of must-haves that plays on a 24-7 loop in the minds of many men. The urge to check off everything on the List is what drives many men away from service to God. The List contains every seductive, delirious worldly goal you ever saw on an episode of *Entourage*:

- Wealth
- Power

- Position
- A hot car
- Great clothes
- A huge crib
- Big toys
- A beautiful, sexy woman on your arm

It's all bling, and it's all hard to get and harder to keep, but that's precisely the point. Men easily lose themselves in conquest, competition, the effort of building something from nothing, lifting themselves above other men. Working through the List becomes a compulsion, because when you have all (or even most) of the above, you've earned that most coveted of labels: success.

THE COST

But it's an illusory kind of success. For proof, look around. We'll bet that you know at least one family that's suffered because the man has put his pursuit of financial, material, and sexual validation over his wife and children. We certainly do. It's a very common story. The problem with the male obsession with the List is that the rewards are transactional—that is, to get something, you have to give up something that you won't get back. For a lot of men, that something is time with their families, their peace of mind, or their very character. For others, it's their physical or mental health.

God made men aggressive, competitive, sexual beings, but He also made them capable of more. The List is a placebo. It makes some men feel like they live in a world where aggression, competition, and uncontrolled carnality are the only keys to getting what they want. Success isn't just professional or sexual, however, but moral, personal, and spiritual. If you fail at these things, they become liabilities that will derail everything you aspire to.

Think about how many men who used to be on top of the world can't even get a job because they had no discipline in their personal lives. Think about how many men are in jail because while society said they were successful, they overlooked everything else to keep checking off the items on the List. Not only do they pay for their lack of discipline, but their children and grandchildren pay for it, too.

To paraphrase, the List is a lie.

There is no List, no catalog of external achievements,
that will make a man more of a man.

Becoming a man—and a husband worthy of the wife God intends for you—requires a deeper understanding.

MEN'S DISCIPLINES

Because men tend to be so sexually driven, the methods to keep men in The Wait need to be fairly . . . extreme. Try some of these:

- *Block the numbers of any women you've been seeing that you aren't serious about.* Make contacting you a lost cause. Rude? Maybe. If you're concerned, text or email the women you really care about in the beginning and tell them what you're doing.

- *Have an accountability buddy.* That's someone you meet with regularly who doesn't let you backslide. It could be a friend, sibling, pastor, or colleague. But make sure it's someone you can talk to who won't let you off the hook.

- *Quit porn.* Yes, even Christian men have been known to look at pornography. Ethical issues aside, it's bad for the willpower. Set up your web browser to block it, and stop tempting yourself.

- *Get involved in something that challenges and improves you.* Join a networking group or basketball league. Hit the gym. Do something that enriches body, mind, and spirit—as well as improves your extracurricular time.

- *Build a stronger prayer life.* We can't stress this enough. Prayer will be your lifeline when you feel weak or when doubts torture your mind. Have a daily prayer practice.

- *Volunteer.* Commit to a church ministry, work with a non-

profit or with fatherless boys. This will focus you on grati-
tude and your own blessings.

WALKING, TALKING SEX DRIVES

An obsession with sex, wealth, and power diminishes men.
That's bad, but what's even worse is that the reckless pursuit
of women demotes many men to little more than walking,
talking libidos—primitive animals barely able to control
their sexual urges and willing to trample everything in their
path just to "get some."

We shouldn't have to explain how offensive and destructive that idea is. God created man in His own image, gifted
with a divine spirit and a mind capable of flights of extraor-
dinary vision and creativity, but an addiction to sex turns
men into something far less than the image of God. Make
no mistake, some men are addicted to sex and women in the
same way that an alcoholic is addicted to liquor. If they don't
have a woman around, they can't cope.

Men's lack of sexual discipline is responsible for a fair
amount of the abuse we see in society. For instance, one in
five women is sexually assaulted while attending college.
The problem has gotten so bad that in 2014 President Obama
launched an initiative called "It's On Us" to combat sexual

assault on campus. From rape to extramarital affairs, a great deal of evil occurs because some men cannot (or choose not to) control their sexual appetites.

Yet with all this, much of our culture still consents to men living with little to no accountability in this area. High schools all over the United States and Canada have—this is so ridiculous that we can hardly stand it—banned girls from wearing leggings, yoga pants, or skinny jeans on the grounds that they're distractions that incite boys to sexual fantasies and turn girls into sex objects. First of all, we're talking about high school kids; male or female, they're thinking about sex a third of the time anyway. That's normal.

But what's disturbing about this sort of thing is that it presumes that males cannot be responsible with their sexual urges—that the only way to prevent men from being aroused is to make sure girls do not wear formfitting clothes. That's not just condescending to men. It's offensive and humiliating.

DEVON: We men have never been taught how to manage our sexuality and sexual appetites—how to train and harness that energy constructively.

The man who recklessly gives himself over to his sex drive denies and distances himself from his divine nature. He courts chaos, drama, legal troubles, illegitimate children—everything this side of the plagues that Moses warned Pharaoh about in Exodus. Worst of all, he becomes manipulative and callous, willing to do or say any-thing to get a woman into bed. He becomes addicted not just to the physical feeling of sex but also to the psychology of how sex makes him feel—and the game he must play to produce this feeling.

Before we go too far with this, let's make one thing clear: we get it. There's nothing wrong with men enjoying the at-tention of women. For some people, that's fun . . . for a while. But before too long, most men find themselves filled with despair over the empty lives they're leading.

If that describes you, then why not commit to stopping the madness? Make a different choice for your life—one that might *save* your life.

DEVON: I'll never forget this vision God gave me. In this vision, I was at the altar of my wedding about to say my vows, when the minister told me to turn around. When I did I saw the center aisle that I had just walked down lit-tered with the fallen bodies of women I had dated. They were writhing and in pain. And then it was like I heard God say, "Was it worth all their pain for you to end up here?" So many times as men, we date selfishly, uncon-cerned about the collateral damage we do to women just so we can find happiness in the moment.

God was telling me, "Don't play with my daughters'

hearts. Stop manipulating them for your own selfish ful-fillment. If you're not serious, then let them know and don't lead them on." This was a powerful vision that changed the way I dated as a man.

WHAT ARE YOU DOING WITH YOUR NOT-TIED-DOWNNESS?

Somewhere between the exhausting frustration of a life spent chasing everything in a skirt and the fulfillment of settling down with one good woman is fear. For many men, obsessing over sex and reducing women to sex objects is a defense against getting pulled into a real relationship and the accompanying terror of losing their freedom.

Tied down. Trapped by the old ball and chain. Take your pick. In the popular imagination, real men are free-range. They come and go with no ties or long-term promises. Once a man gets tangled up with one woman (says the stereotype), he's doomed to a boring, soulless domestic life with kids, a mortgage, and sex with the same woman for the rest of his life. For a man raised on the idea of conquest and competition, who's been living the life of a player, the loss of freedom might look like living death.

But honestly, how much freedom do these men really

have? If you ask one hundred habitually single guys why they're uninterested in commitment, you'll hear a lot of talk about wanting to get further in life and career. They're in love with the idea of freedom in the future, but not its possibilities for today. It's fine to not want to be tied down, but what are you doing with your not-tied-downness?

Hmm, it seems like we've hit the heart of the matter. If you're a man who's not doing anything with his alleged freedom but chasing one empty liaison after another, are you really free? Or are you enslaved to this type of behavior that controls your every move? God created woman to be part of man, to evoke the best in man, to help you become the best man you can be. Having the right woman in your life will make you a better man. Also, the right woman will bring you closer to your goals, not push you away from them.

"NO" BEFORE BROS

There's a lot of validation and pleasure in being part of a female-chasing pack of dudes. You get camaraderie, approval of your skills, and a built-in wingman on a Saturday night. It's appealing. Understood.

But here's the secret no one's talking about: almost every player knows that what he's doing is unhealthy and disrespectful to himself and women (because if another man was doing the same thing to his mother, sister, or daughter, he wouldn't stand for it). Guys know, deep down, that chasing sexual pleasure diminishes them and debases women. They just won't say it. The pressure of the pack—to fit in and get that fist-bump, you're-the-man approval—is powerful.

But if you're going to practice The Wait and do it right, you need to step up and be the leader. Say what none of your brothers will say: this isn't good for you and you're opting out. You're going celibate to prove that you're more than your sex drive. The guys will laugh it off as a joke at first, of course. Then they'll be shocked and a little upset. Some might withdraw their validation, and you might panic and feel the need to retract your resolve.

Don't. Stick to your guns. Men respect strength, even if it's in something they disagree with. Your real friends will back your play and respect you more for sticking to it, even if they don't get

it. Once they see how it's giving you the time and focus to get
your mind right, excel in your career, and get in shape, who will be
laughing then?

Contrary to what you might think, those situations aren't
hopeless.

WHO IS YOUR WIFE?

Of course, we're talking about the wife in the same way that
we talked about the husband in the previous chapter. Your
wife is more than the woman whose finger you put a ring on.
She's the perfect fit for your best male qualities, the point to
your counterpoint. Your wife is the woman God intends you
to be with, and she may be nothing at all like the women you
once chased (or still chase) for their looks or the promise of
another one-night stand. Your wife is:

- Careful consideration and common sense tempering
  your bull-facing-the-red-cape impulsivity. She cools
  you off, calms you down, and helps you see the whole
  picture before you attack the situation.
- The one who calls out immature man-boy nonsense
  and reminds you that you're better than that. She challenges you to step up and be everything you can be.

- The partner who loves your passionate, big-idea, change-the-world nature and embraces your aggressive desire to build a better life for both of you. She helps you understand that raw energy, channel it, and use it to create the future.

- Your spiritual guide. Women aren't taught to force the action, so they tend to be more open to their inner lives, including conversing with the Lord. Your wife can help you listen to that soft inner voice.

- A counterweight to your masculine brute force. She possesses persuasiveness and subtlety. If you can't get what you want through a hostile takeover, what about a handshake?

Once you see that your fear of losing your freedom is an illusion, you'll start to appreciate how finding your wife can enhance not only your spiritual life but your material life and every measure of personal success.

DEVON: Having Meagan as my wife has not only made me a better man but better at my profession, too. She's tempered my judgment with her own, and I've learned to see choices through the filter of not only my own experience but hers as well. She's a strong woman who knows her own mind, and her strength has meant that I don't have to be strong all the time. It is a great relief as a man to know that she can handle things at times when I might not be able to.

Until I found my wife, I didn't appreciate how much the right woman would help God's plan for my life develop. That's true for all men, I think. We're like raw energy or a raging river that needs to be challenged and channeled so it can change things for the better. That's what Meagan has done for me, and that's what a good man's wife does for him.

You might not be able to notice your wife because you're being blinded by sexual desires. That's why it's so important for men to practice The Wait. If you're a mature man who's open to change, playing the field begins to lose its allure when you start noticing truly attractive qualities in women. After you've been with enough physically attractive women who don't fulfill you intellectually or spiritually, the game loses its allure. You begin to discover that smart, confident women who know what they want and don't need a man to feel complete are irresistible. You can detect these qualities clearly and quickly when you're not chasing sex all the time.

How can you find your wife? The surest way is to become the kind of man she'll be attracted to—self-aware, mature, and in tune with God's vision for your life. Keep in mind one lesson of our courtship, though: your wife won't always be the type of woman you think you want. You could be convinced that you will never be interested in someone older than you, until a great woman ten years your senior knocks you off your feet.

Have faith and be open to women of all ages, races, backgrounds, and habits. You don't know when or how God will bring your wife to your attention.

THE WAIT AND . . . BUSINESS

The mythology of men and the mythology of business are predicated on the same testosterone-soaked idea: real men make things happen. They force the action. They seize the initiative. Can you smell the machismo?

However, business has a lot more in common with the discipline of The Wait than men realize. For one thing, you can't control the market. You can only do great things and make sure people know about them, then wait for good stuff to happen. Also, you can't try to please everyone.

In the world of The Wait and the world of business, excellence and dedication always produce results, even if the results take time. In The Wait, you work on your character, mind, and spirit knowing that when you're ready, God will bring the right woman your way. In business, you produce quality and provide great value for their own sake, knowing that if you do it long enough, customers will come.

FAITH AND THE WAITING MAN

Faith can pose a problem even for men who have tired of dating multiple women. Many men lack patience. We don't like to wait for things to come to us. We don't wait, period.

But that's a trap. Distractions may reduce the temptation to have sex, but if your focus is not on the patience required to grow your faith, you're not going to do the deep personal work you need to be ready for the woman you're meant to be with. Money, sex, possessions, position, and title distract us from spiritual development. Eventually, you need to stop and go toe to toe with the hard questions:

- What do I want?
- Why am I not happy?
- What is my purpose?

Men often bulldoze through such questions instead of sitting with them, getting to know them. Our culture discourages vulnerability, introspection, and doubt in men. These qualities are perceived as weakness. Boys don't cry, we're told. A lot of guys suppress their fears and needs, and then that dam breaks when they're in their forties or fifties and they have no idea how to handle it. They know no other way to express themselves other than through anger, power, and control. We've been sold an image of men that's damaging men.

The catch about finding your wife is that becoming a worthy husband means embracing vulnerability, introspection, and doubt. Men have the potential to be just as healing, noble, nurturing, and high-minded as women if they hold themselves to a higher standard. That doesn't mean becoming less of a man or becoming more like a woman. It means becoming a different kind of man, one who can shed the Neanderthal mentality of his younger years for greater wisdom, restraint, tenderness, and faith. This means finally leaving the adolescent boy behind and embracing the power of real manhood. There's nothing weak or unmanly about that.

Still, a lot of men have trouble with this, and the reason is a lack of faith. Like we said earlier, fear is a failure of faith. Programmed to be stubbornly self-reliant, men rebel against the notion that waiting will allow God to bring them what they want. Either that, or they don't feel worthy of what God's got in mind, so they go out and make their own "life."

Career, possessions, and sex will not bring peace. Love, purpose, connection, joy—those are things only God can bring us, and for him to do that, we've got to slow down long enough to see what's in our path. Men crave motion; waiting requires being still and listening. If men can find a way to quell that restlessness and weakness of faith long enough to stop and pay attention, they'll see God work wonders in their lives.

That takes trust, and trust doesn't come easily to a lot of men. Men who learn to trust God learn one of the most valuable lessons in life: you might not always be able to trust yourself, but you can always trust God. As men, we love to believe in our strength, but the truth is that we aren't as strong as we think. We think we're being strong in relying on only our own resources and no one else, and then we're surprised when we fall. For men, true strength comes when we allow ourselves to be vulnerable and weak, dependent on God. As you come into practicing The Wait, you may find your discipline and strength to be wanting. Accept that while you're finding greater discipline and strength, God is there for you. He won't ever abandon you. He's got your back.

ATTENTION IS THE CURRENCY OF TRUE SUCCESS

Men who become stronger in The Wait will quickly discover something they weren't expecting: The Wait has incredible practical benefits. When you're spending a lot of your time, money, and energy chasing women and sex, you can't operate at full capacity. But as a man, part of what drives you is your ability to be successful in the world, to fulfill your purpose.

Men desire as much control over their world and their place in it as possible. The tool to gain control is *attention*— where you focus your will at any given moment. If you want to change or control something, you have to "pay" attention to it. Attention is the currency of success. But even the smartest, most gifted man has only so much attention to spend. There's only so much time in the day, only so much mental bandwidth. The more you spend your attention on pursuits like casual sex, the less you have to "buy" the outcomes you really want—to become the man you know you can truly be.

For men, the foundation for success is built on sexual and romantic discipline. Attending to the drama and keeping up with all your different identities is distracting you from the work you need to do on your character, spirituality, and intellect. If you're constantly preoccupied with calling women, keeping them happy, and ducking relationships gone toxic, you probably don't even know what work you need to do!

With The Wait, that changes. You'll be like a cluttered house where the windows have been opened and 90 percent of the furniture has been moved out. Suddenly, there's room to breathe, think, and stretch. Waiting clears headspace for you to focus on the pursuits that make you a better man, a better lawyer, a better athlete, a better businessman.

Can real men wait? Absolutely, and they do.

TAKE INVENTORY

How to begin? Take advantage of a natural male trait: a taste for extreme action and dramatic jumps into the unknown. Take women completely out of the picture for a while. Maybe stop dating for a time. Delete the Black Book app from your phone. Tell the guys you're not going to the usual hangouts anymore. It won't be easy at first, but you'll be amazed at how much time you have to focus on the things you really want in life when you're not chasing sex and the drama that can come with it. You'll be amazed at how much positive change you'll experience in your life.

Too much? Okay, then start with the core of The Wait. Be celibate for one week (or a day, if even a week seems impossible) and see how it goes. Then add one more week. Use prayer to keep you centered. Practice self-control and discipline by working out and engaging in other things in life you enjoy doing. Identify a pattern of behavior in your dating life that causes you the most headaches and fix it ASAP. Write down your intentions for waiting and stick to them. Once you start seeing some real benefits—for instance, less stress and more peace and focus—you'll have become a believer in the value of waiting.

Most important, just as we suggested for women, do a personal inventory built around the same five key questions:

- What have I been spending my energy and attention on and why?
- What have I been compromising to do that?

- Is what I'm doing filling me up or emptying me out?
- What is the driving force in my choices?
- What am I ready to sacrifice in order to change things and become my best self?

You'll have to sacrifice plenty in order to wait. But that's okay. The Wait gives men permission not to stoop to the expectations of others. It absolves men of the need to reinforce the male stereotype. And anyway, after a while, the whole peacocking thing really loses its appeal. Every child of God has an innate desire to do more and be more. So get to it, man.

WISE WAITING

There's plenty you can do with the spare time and money you used to spend on buying clothes and accessories, going to clubs, picking up women, and dodging angry post-sex calls and text messages:

- Go to church consistently.
- Visit parents and old friends.
- Read.
- Work out.
- Focus on your career advancement.
- Launch a business.
- Learn to meditate.
- Get a pet.
- Learn to cook.
- Try new restaurants.
- Start writing that book that you've been putting off.
- Live in the present moment.

CHAPTER SEVEN

CAN I DATE WHILE I WAIT?

*To say that one waits a lifetime for his soulmate to come
around is a paradox. People eventually get sick of waiting, take a chance on someone, and by the art of commitment become soulmates, which takes a lifetime to perfect.*
—CRISS JAMI, *VENUS IN ARMS*

You're practicing The Wait. You're celibate. You're working on yourself in body, mind, and spirit. But you're
bored. You don't want to sit at home or spend all your time at
the gym, at work, or at church. You want to have some fun.
So you're asking questions. Should I date right now? When
is God going to bring the right person? When is someone
going to ask me out? When am I going to meet "the One"?

These are the questions that plague you when you're
single. Don't worry, they plagued us, too. Let's be honest, the
longer these questions go unanswered, the more depressed

we tend to become. How do we remain patient with the process yet active while we're waiting?

The answer is definitely *not* "don't date." That's not what we're suggesting at all. You can date while you're practicing The Wait. You just can't date in the same way you did before.

This is where it's critical to remember that The Wait is not just about sex. The principles behind The Wait—productive patience, listening to God, working on perfecting yourself, and letting good things happen—will benefit you in all areas of your relationships and your life as a whole. Dating is a perfect example. Even if you're practicing The Wait and remaining celibate, you need to assess if you and the person you're dating have passion. You'll need it if you want your marriage to be successful. Letting sex wait allows you to evaluate all the aspects of your attraction—physical, intellectual, emotional, and spiritual—and figure out if your chemistry is real and has the potential to last.

WHAT DO YOU DESERVE?

Now, it's true that when you're beginning to wait, it can be really beneficial to take some time to be alone and get used to the idea of not having sex and resisting temptation. This is a time to take stock of who you are, what you want, and why you've been having relationship troubles. That's wisdom. The world isn't going to end if you excuse yourself from the dating scene for a while. The right girls or guys will still be out there. But before you rejoin them, answer three very important questions for yourself:

- What relationship pattern do I want to break?
- What kind of person do I want in my life?
- What do I deserve?

The last one is the most important. We ask ourselves what we want, but we rarely ask ourselves what we deserve. When we forget to ask, we're more likely to approach relationships from a place of need and insufficiency. We need to be with someone because we fear being alone. We can't end a relationship that causes us pain because we worry that no one else will want us—we feel insufficient. Or perhaps we feel that hurt and conflict are what we deserve, a common state of mind for people healing from pain or trauma.

If you've spent years dating the same messed-up people, putting up with the same drama, and recovering from the same hysterical fights and awful breakups, ask yourself why. Was it because you felt, deep down, that was all you deserved? We're here to tell you that you deserve more. You're a child of God. You're naturally a source of love and light, an important player in manifesting God's will in the world—if you'll let yourself see it! You deserve respect, fulfillment, joy, and the kind of profound, real love that only comes when you get to know someone's spirit and when you love yourself enough to let them love you.

What do you deserve? Love? Respect? Someone who will bring out the best in you and inspire you to bring out the best in them? Dating—carefully—while practicing The Wait is a terrific way to start finding some of the answers.

IT'S CONFUSING

Still, dating when you're in that place where God comes first can be mighty confusing. It was for us. We were both at a place in our lives where we were listening to God's voice and trying to remain open to what He was sending us, but even then, when He did everything but hit us over the head, we weren't sure what to do.

MEAGAN: After a while, I started speaking my knowledge about DeVon. I told my friend Tasha Smith, "I have to tell you something. God told me that DeVon's my husband."

She supportively smiled and then said, "Praise God, you know he's celibate, right?"

I said, "Well, I'm celibate, too."

She said, "No, he's for-real celibate. And you know he's a preacher, too, right?"

I didn't know that, and to be honest I'm glad I didn't. Because if I had, it probably would have scared me away. But during those months, I settled into celibacy, focusing on healing, letting God work through me, and separating those people who weren't good for me from my life. At one point, I told my godsister, Kimberly, about DeVon. She said, "Does he know he's your husband?"

I said, "No, but I know, because God told me."

Then came the premiere of *Jumping the Broom* in May 2011. My girlfriends and I were running around the party trying to find DeVon, because by this time I'd told all my close friends about the revelation I believed I'd gotten from God. They wanted to meet "this DeVon guy" for themselves! So as we were going upstairs to the second floor of the party, he and his aunts were coming downstairs. I remember feeling like a little schoolgirl caught on my way to catch a glimpse of her crush.

Later, at the party after the premiere, one of the guests was talking me to death. DeVon texted me and I replied, "Help!" We decided to meet outside and talk. That was when I began to see the revelation God gave me coming to life.

DEVON: I was busy doing the promotion for my first book, *Produced by Faith,* which was set to come out the same week that *Jumping the Broom* premiered. I did an event in Riverside, California, at Mt. Rubidoux, a church where I often preach, and Meagan and Laz Alonso were kind enough to come out and talk about the movie as well as give insight into their careers and faith. I had no idea that Meagan already considered me to be her husband. I was glad she came, but I wasn't thinking anything romantic.

It's funny, because a few months before this event, my cousins Troy and LaFawn, who live in Las Vegas, had told me, "Because of all that's going on in your life, you're going to marry somebody famous, high profile."

I scoffed. "No way. You all are crazy." That was not something I wanted at all.

Well, Troy and LaFawn were at this event at Mt. Rubidoux, and afterward they came up to me, pointed to Meagan, and said, "That's her. She's the one."

I was floored. I said, "What? No, you don't know what you're talking about." I did not want to date an actress, much less marry one! Then my mother and my cousin Staci said something similar. They both were like, "What was going on with you and Meagan onstage? We think she likes you." I thought all of them had been drinking (LOL) or were just completely out of their minds, because I didn't see that at all. But they were right; there was definitely an emotional and spiritual connection between Meagan and me that I couldn't see.

Then the premiere of *Jumping the Broom* came. My family was there and we were having a great time. I ran into Meagan on the stairs and we ended up taking a picture with my mom, my brother, and a few aunts. *Wow, Lord, was that a hint? Meagan in a photo with my family?* But I was still oblivious.

Finally, as the party was dying down, the uncertainty got the best of me. I decided to see if something was really up with us. I texted her. Immediately, she replied, "Help!" I went downstairs and we met outside in the courtyard of the party and started talking. The deeper we got into conversation, the more people started coming over and interrupting us. So I told her we'd have to wait and finish our conversation in a few weeks, after I finished my book tour.

DUI: DATING UNDER INFATUATION

If there's one thing our story should make clear, it's that being in The Wait does not mean you'll know what to do when you meet someone amazing. In fact, meeting someone like that could make waiting harder! What do you do? Do you date this person? Do you wait for God to tell you what to do? We definitely come down on the side of getting out there and testing the waters—carefully. When in doubt, go out. But do it armed with this knowledge.

Infatuation (or sometimes what we think is love) can be an addictive substance. It's amazing to feel that rush of hormones and that electricity when you meet, touch, or kiss someone for the first time. Like songs and movies have said before us, infatuation is a drug. Infatuation is defined as an intense but short-lived passion or admiration for someone. The problems start when we let the effects of infatuation, not our reason and character, dictate our actions. That's when we make reckless, foolish, self-destructive choices—over and over and over again. Sometimes you can get so infatuated with someone and you think it's real love, but instead of waiting to evaluate this you move too fast with that person. By the time infatuation wears off, you're in so deep, it's hard to get out.

Bad daters are, essentially, infatuation addicts. Do you have a friend who's constantly repeating the same awful behavior with girls or guys? We'll bet you do; everybody has at least one. (Hint: If you don't have one, odds are you *are* the one.) This person always seems to be hurtling from one doomed relationship to another, never looking before he or she leaps, always eager to surrender to the feelings that come when things are just starting out, always getting his or her heart broken and more often than not, crying on your shoulder. Does this pattern look familiar?

1. Your friend cleans up the mess after a tormented, horrible breakup and swears never to make the same mistakes again.

2. Your friend meets someone new and after an unnervingly short period, insists that it's love.

3. You or others spot serious red flags about the person, but when you mention them (and remind your friend about the pledge not to repeat past relationship blunders), he or she gets angry and insists this person is the One.

4. The infatuation passes and things go south: fights, lying, reading text messages, accusations, the whole horror show.

5. The inevitable nasty breakup happens, leaving your friend hurt and shattered—and if this has been going on long enough, possibly straining your friendship.

Most of us have done it at one time or another. Some do it for years before finally waking up and realizing that they're on drugs. DUI in this book means "Dating Under Infatuation": the jumpy shot of adrenaline we get when he touches our arm, the warm rush we feel when she smiles at us from across the room.

That's sweet and seductive, but it ain't love.

Love is deeper, more mature, and subtler. When we confuse it with infatuation and sexual chemistry, we waste years chasing shadows, trying to satisfy our need for certainty or validation, and blinding ourselves to how God is trying to bless us.

TYPE OR TYPO?

A big part of The Wait is about breaking old patterns, and one of those patterns has to do with your type. As in the type of person you've typically dated. You know: blondes or guys with goatees, career women or bad boys. We all have a few types we're drawn to.

The trouble with types is that they're really stereotypes. They're not real people; they're just qualities that we want in our lives. But when you focus on type, you date a caricature, not a person, so those relationships are doomed.

Try deliberately dating out of your type and see what happens. If you've always been attracted to tall guys, try dating shorter ones. If you've always been attracted to women with long hair, give one with short hair a shot. What have you got to lose? The type you've been dating hasn't led to anything lasting, so it's worth trying something new.

THE JURY IS OUT

Because it's so tempting to confuse the flush and rush of a kiss with love, dating while waiting demands a fresh approach to the social scene. If you want to meet people and enjoy yourself, you need to adopt what we call the jury-box mentality.

If you've been on a jury, you know what we mean. If you haven't, we'll explain. When you sit on a jury, every time you leave the courtroom the judge will instruct you not to draw any conclusions about the case. You're not supposed to decide innocence or guilt until all the evidence is in. You're expected to remain in a state of nonjudgment.

That's exactly the way you should be dating when you're in The Wait. Like we said earlier, people really, really want to fall in love. But infatuation clouds our reason and impairs our ability to make good decisions. Falling for somebody makes it harder to look at them critically, see flaws, and ask important questions like "Do you want kids one day?" or "How did your last relationship end?" How often have you let yourself be so blinded by infatuation that you've ignored or excused a lover's serious transgressions, only to kick yourself later? We've all done it.

In The Wait, you stop that endless loop by delaying the gratification of letting yourself fall head over heels before you really know the other person. Instead, you venture into the dating scene with a jury mentality, observing and learning but not judging. You maintain a healthy level of detachment. You don't commit to anyone prematurely. That doesn't mean you can't have fun. It means that you don't rush to judge someone as being perfect or the One based on a few encounters, a few dates, or even a few church services together.

To do this, you don't have to know exactly what you want from a relationship. All you have to do is date with the confidence that you are a terrific catch and faith that God will pair you with the right person when you and the time are right.

Waiting is about keeping a cool head, analyzing the situation, and staying rational. Despite the pressure and our desire to be in love and be loved, you're choosing to see how things play out before you make a decision about whether this person is or isn't right for you. This lets you in on an incredibly powerful relationship secret:

People will eventually reveal themselves if you allow them to.

Often, we conspire with people to keep them from showing us who they really are. We fall in love with an idea of who we want someone to be, but we don't allow time and space for them to *show* us who they are.

We know some incredible actors, but we've discovered some of the greatest acting goes on in relationships. People play the part of the supportive boyfriend or caring girlfriend, but it's just an act. Trouble is, by the time we get the memo, we're so deep into the relationship that it's hard—even damaging—to back out.

In this new jury-box mentality, you'll hold on to your ability to see potential partners clearly—gifts, faults, and all. You'll slow things down. You won't commit too soon. You'll put your own needs first, which is exactly what you should do. And you'll retain the self-control to say good-bye to anyone who doesn't meet your standards, doesn't treat you with respect, or infects your life with their drama. To put it another way, you become a smart juror in the trial of your life.

YOU KNOW NOT BECAUSE YOU ASK NOT

The trick here is to stay engaged in getting to know someone you're dating but remain objective. By staying objective, you also gain the ability to ask the right questions of potential partners.

Think of it like the process of buying a house, similar to a concept Bishop T. D. Jakes references in his best-selling book *Before You Do*. You don't run into the first house you see and buy it without doing an inspection first; it's too big an investment. You go through an intense, tedious process of questions, evaluations, appraisals, and so on to determine if the house is worth the cost.

You've got to approach dating the same way. You can still

dance and kiss and hold hands and enjoy being together. But part of you should always have your eyes wide open for tell-tales, good and bad, that give you clues into the person's character, personality, and perceptions so you can determine if there is genuine compatibility. You're shopping, not buying.

If the relationship looks promising, don't be afraid to start asking questions. This is where many relationships fail. Many fear asking questions: "What if the other person gets upset by the things I want to know?" If someone you're dating or considering dating gets angry about honest questions, they may have something to hide. Beware.

It's your responsibility to get clarity on whether or not this person is the right one for you, so don't be afraid to ask—and keep asking. When the two of us first started dating, our biggest questions were about what we wanted out of life:

- What were our goals?
- Were we at a place where we wanted to get married?
- Where did we see our lives going?
- What was important to us?

We were both open and honest in our responses. One of the reasons our relationship is so strong is because we started off with an open conversation about these questions and our expectations . . . and kept that conversation going. Honesty connected us and kept us focused not on the physical but on really getting to know each other.

Have these conversations early so you don't waste your time if you and the other person aren't compatible. There's nothing shallow or manipulative about that. If you're not right for each other, it's best to know it immediately. You don't go down that road, falling for that person and wasting your time. You stay on the right road and keep nurturing what matters.

Now, there's a difference between asking genuine questions that are relevant and asking questions that are just nosy. Here's what we mean. One of the touchiest subjects in any relationship—dating or married—is the other person's past. We are curious creatures and we want to know who the other person may have slept with, who they have dated, and so on. There is no standard rule about whether it's okay to ask or answer these questions. However, we're in Pandora's-box territory now. Before asking questions about your partner's past, ask yourself:

- Is the information relevant?
- Can I handle the truth?
- Will the information bring us closer together or drive us apart?

We've seen many relationships break up because the individuals didn't stop and think before they began to pry. This was a touchy subject for us as well. Because we both work in the same industry and traditionally have dated within that industry, it was likely that we'd know people we had each dated. So we made an informed, mutual decision: we would share certain, but not all, aspects of our dating past. This way, neither of us would be put in a situation of feeling disrespected if we ended up working with the other's ex.

To this day we have not discussed with each other every single person we've dated. It isn't relevant. That kind of information can plant seeds of judgment, anger, frustration, and jealousy. Bottom line, we trust each other. If there is something that hasn't yet been shared, we know it will come out if it becomes relevant.

Asking questions when dating is critical, but so is knowing which questions to ask and which ones *not* to ask.

BEWARE OF YOUR LIST

Tear up your List. We talked in chapter six about the List for success that most men have. But there's another kind. That checklist that details everything about the One: what they will look like, how tall they will be, how much money they will make, what race they will be, everything that represents your ideal person down to hair color, eye color, weight, body type, occupation, personality, and more.

Here's the thing: we all know that *nobody* is going to check every box on that List. But that doesn't stop us from looking for someone who does! By looking for characteristics instead of people, we often prematurely accept or reject potential partners based on traits that might wind up being unimportant if we got to know them better as people.

Are you really open to the right person even if the right person checks none of the boxes on your List? Will you be open to love no matter how God chooses to bring it to you? What if love comes as someone from a race you've never dated before? Will you consider and accept it or will you reject it? It's quite possible the kind of person you think you should be attracted to might differ from the person you actually are attracted to.

This problem surfaced for us because God put love into packages very different from what either of us expected. While it obviously didn't keep us from getting together, it did raise doubts and cause some conflict. It was also a wake-up call.

DEVON: On our first date, Meagan asked if we could go out on the patio so she could have a smoke. I was asking myself, "Lord, what in the world are you doing?" I was way out of my comfort zone, because smoking was a top *no* on my List. It wasn't just that Meagan's smoking caught me by surprise. She was also an actress and had a reputation as a party girl. There were other things on my List of nonstarters.

Well, you know what they say: God loves to make a man break a vow. Here was God, asking me to overlook important things on my List. To get to know *her*—not her bad habits or other people's perception of who she was—I had to have faith.

I prayed and sought God's wisdom and the counsel of one of my good friends, and I decided that I would hang in there, take a chance on getting to know and understand her. This ended up being one of the best decisions I ever made.

MEAGAN: In the past, I had always felt that the people I was dating never really saw me. They may have found me attractive, and we may have been happy, there may even have been genuine love, but in the end I always felt like I was never really being accepted fully for who I was. When I went into my season of waiting, I wanted someone to see me the way God saw me.

Now, as I mentioned before, when God revealed to me that DeVon was going to be my husband, I didn't realize that in addition to working in entertainment, he was a preacher. Not that I ever had anything against men in ministry, but it wasn't exactly high on my List. I knew that being in ministry comes with a lot of scrutiny and judgment, yet I needed to get to know who he was as a man and not let my preconceived notions of "preacher" stop me from doing that.

As we mentioned earlier, our second date was so special. We were at a Prince concert at the House of Blues on the Sunset Strip. We sat outside talking and DeVon started telling me who he knew that I was—not who he or others *thought* I was, but who he *knew* I was. Most people have a preconceived notion of me and never look deep enough to see my heart. That was always a source of pain for me. But he was so sincere, and I could feel that in my spirit because of the clarity The Wait provided. I would say, "Well, this is what other people see," and he would say, "But that's not who you are." He just took me apart.

My mother and sisters have had a lifetime to understand what DeVon understood after two dates. He made me cry; it meant so much for him to see who I truly was at heart.

As we began dating during our Wait, we learned more about each other, and it became clear there was chemistry and compatibility. That's dating from The Wait perspective:

being open and not rushing the process of getting to know someone. You ask questions and find out about the person in a healthy and mature way. You don't overcommit, but you don't close yourself off, either.

DEVON: The Wait gave me so much clarity. I could discern who Meagan was, and as I got a chance to know her, it felt like I already knew her. I'd seen her act and admired her talent, and I knew she was sweet, but I discovered, "There's a lot more here than people realize. There's a dynamic, powerful, compassionate, God-fearing woman here."

As I got to know Meagan, she told me why and how she had picked up the smoking habit and expressed her strong desire to quit. Over time, I realized that smoking was a bad habit, but it wasn't tethered to the essence of who Meagan was. Drinking's a behavior. Smoking's a behavior. It's not the God-given essence of a person. If someone doesn't have the right integrity, personality, or character for you, then the fact that they might be a nonsmoking vegan becomes irrelevant. There's nothing wrong with having ideas about what you want and don't want in a mate, but don't confuse behaviors on your List with the qualities that make up the essence of a person. Behaviors can change; essence won't.

MEAGAN: Even though DeVon and I are very similar, in some areas we are very different. We both saw things about each other that we would have preferred to be different. But we worked through it in a healthy way. The smartest thing we did was to learn about each other and accept each other as who we were. Over time, in some of those areas we did actually change, but it was a natural change that happened in its own time and without force.

When you begin to free yourself from being so rigidly attached to your List, you realize that once you find someone God has for you, someone you connect with on an emotional, intellectual, practical, and spiritual level, this is the foundation of real, unconditional love.

In the end, we learned a powerful lesson:

Unconditional love means accepting someone for who they are now, not who you hope they will be one day.

People don't change on demand. And you can't change someone; they have to want to change. The confidence of knowing whom God is bringing to you gives you the patience and confidence to say, "Okay, Lord, I can wait because I know this is all happening for a reason."

DIPPING YOUR TOE INTO THE DATING POOL

Ready to wade back into dating? Becoming liberated from your List and remaining objective about potential partners are both good pieces of advice no matter what your dating life looks like. But there are multiple stages to anyone's dating experience, and The Wait is a little different for each one. We want to address two specific areas:

1. Not dating (whether voluntarily or involuntarily)
2. Dating (but not yet in a committed relationship)

In the first stage, maybe you've spent several months purposefully steering clear of the dating scene. You've hung out with some friends, but that's all. You're waiting but not by choice, or you're in a self-imposed time of waiting. Maybe you've made it a point not to date anyone, to spend the time you once dedicated to the pursuit of the opposite sex on examining your mistakes, figuring out what you want, and discovering what you deserve. You've been praying, taking classes, and getting healthy. But now you're ready to jump back in.

Great. Go for it. Some tips on how to begin while you also practice The Wait:

Keep your focus inward and upward. An outward focus is

all about noticing surface features that you find attractive: physical appearance, great style, and so on. This is the time to put "I am" before "I want" and let God show you the worthwhile people you need to meet.

Go about dating the same way you'd go about looking for a job. Get out there, be active, and be consistent. Dating takes practice, and dating with a Wait mind-set even more so. The more you meet new people and practice evaluating them objectively, the better you'll get at it.

Don't be afraid to use dating services. There's nothing wrong with trying everything from eHarmony and Match.com to It's Just Lunch. You never know how God might use one of these avenues to help you meet the right person.

Be patient. You might have to spend time with a lot of people before you find one who sees you for who you really are. You might be tempted to change yourself to get someone's approval. Don't. Changing yourself for someone else's approval is not something you can live with long-term. When you finally find someone who gets you, everything changes.

Be strong. You'll be tempted to fall back into old dating habits—obsessing over when he'll call, one-night stands, committing too fast—but don't. Be aware of them and keep your commitment to The Wait and celibacy.

STEADY AT YOUR CENTER

Like we've said, because you're back on the market doesn't mean you stop waiting. You're just staying objective, rational, and observant while you're going out with people. Here are some tips for being successful at that:

- Protect your own time. Studies have shown that people eat more snacks from a clear jar than they do from an opaque one. Point: we want what we see. Even if you like the other person a lot, make sure you protect your space. Have your own independent life. The balance is healthy and it'll help you stay objective.

- Journal your thoughts daily. Seeing your thoughts about your dating life in writing gives you clarity. Write down your opinions, questions, and concerns every day before you turn in. Reread them in the morning.

- Pray. Talk to God daily during The Wait. His voice will remind you just what you're trying to achieve and give you the strength to stick with your plan.

- Reflect on what you're trying to accomplish. It's easy to get lost in a new relationship. Remember what The Wait is about: slowing down, learning, discovering the other person, and finding the partner God has in mind for you. Recalling this can recharge your discipline to be patient and stay cool.

GOING DEEPER

Say you've been going out, exploring your options but remaining noncommittal. You've done really well, in fact, at being choosier and not asking anybody out in a panic just so you don't have to be alone. You've socialized, had some laughs, and gotten or even given out a few phone numbers. Great. But now you've met someone smart, deep, and spiritual. You'd like to ask him or her out. What now?

Talk. Take your communication to the next level. Start asking the important questions we mentioned earlier in the chapter. What do you want out of life? What's your relationship with God? What do you want from your partner? What will you always stand up for? What will you never tolerate?

There's a reason the experts cite communication as one of the keys to a lasting relationship. Communication is everything. Your time is valuable, and you shouldn't waste it on people who don't deserve it. From the first connection and conversation, try to determine if this person is worth more of your time.

Share. Maintain your healthy skepticism, but be open and respect the other person's need to know as much about you as you do about him or her.

Use every date as a learning opportunity. You're refining your perceptions and learning to ask better questions. You're learning more about what you like and what you don't like in this person.

Be honest. If you know you're not genuinely interested, don't date someone just for the sake of it. Don't play with others' feelings. What you sow, you reap.

Make sure you're spiritually on the same page. Someone who doesn't share your values and morals is probably not going to be very compatible with you in the long term.

Make sure the person stimulates you intellectually. Eventually, the desire to rip each other's clothes off will fade, and if you can't light your fire with wit, intelligence, and humor, you've got nothing.

Don't project what you want onto the other person. If you're desperate to be in a committed relationship, you're more likely to ignore flaws and rationalize away unacceptable qualities. Then six months into the relationship you say, "You're not who I thought you were." Whose fault is that?

Look at how your potential partner treats other people. Someone who's infatuated with you or wants you sexually will treat you well, but if they treat other people badly, that's how they're going to treat you when the infatuation wears off.

Make sure the person respects you and values your time. Being late or being on the phone or constantly texting while you are together could be a sign the person doesn't respect you. Relationships have their peaks and valleys, and there will be times when you're just not into each other. During those times, what's going to keep you together is the level of respect you have for each other.

Don't hesitate to hit the eject button if things don't feel right. Trust how you feel in your spirit. If something about the person seems off, it's okay to put things on hold until you feel better about the situation. If you never do, stay away.

Discipline and objectivity will empower you to avoid past mistakes and the pain they caused.

TELLING YOUR DATE ABOUT THE WAIT

There's one more issue at hand as you toe the cliff above dating's treacherous waters: telling your dates about your commitment to waiting. If you feel convicted to practice The Wait, you've got to tell the people you're dating about it. That brings up the possibility that you could be rejected because of it. Some men and women won't be supportive. You need to have faith that if someone doesn't want to be part of what you're doing, that person isn't someone you would have had long-term success with anyway.

But look at it this way: if you're committed to The Wait, telling a prospective partner about The Wait is a terrific screening tool. Some might say that they respect what you're doing but then try to change your mind. Others might get it, ask you about it, and embrace it. Those are the ones with whom something long-term becomes possible.

Remember, The Wait is about being together in that place of nonjudgment and objectivity. It's about stimulating each other intellectually, getting to know each other, and finding common interests that you can experience together. That's how you find a stable place where a relationship can develop into something blessed and lasting.

WISE WAITING

When you tell the person you're dating that you're practicing The Wait, even if they're cool with it, that's no reason to lose your objectivity. People change their minds. They try something and decide it's not for them. Keep your cool and say to yourself, "They're into it. That's great. Let's see how things are in a couple of months." If a few months go by and they are still on board about The Wait, it's okay to celebrate (a little).

CHAPTER EIGHT

WHEN SHOULD I COMMIT?

We have to recognize that there cannot be relationships unless there is commitment, unless there is loyalty, unless there is love, patience, persistence.
—DR. CORNEL WEST

We started dating in May 2011 and by September it was clear that we were on the road to real commitment, to marriage. As part of our mutual commitment to cultivate our spiritual selves instead of our sexual selves, we had decided to go on a Daniel-type fast for forty days, fasting from things like meat, bread, and sweets (Daniel 1:8–16). We wanted God to bring us closer together, as we believed we were moving toward eventually getting engaged. We also wanted clarity, vision, and direction for our lives overall.

Right around that time we learned about an online com-

patibility assessment called PREAPARE/ENRICH (www
.prepare-enrich.com) for couples who are thinking about
becoming engaged. PREPARE/ENRICH is the leading
relationship-inventory and skill-building program used na-
tionally and internationally. It is built on a solid research
foundation and significantly improves a couple's relationship.
It is custom tailored to a couple's relationship and provides
couple exercises to build their relationship skills. You both
independently complete online assessments, and then you
find a counselor in your area to interpret the results and talk
with you about any issues you might need to work out before
you consider marriage. So we did it.

Our counselor told us that we had tested at the highest
level of compatibility—in fact, we were one of the most compatible couples she'd met. That was great news, but it was
only the beginning. We spent the next four months in pre-
engagement counseling with her. About once a week, we met
and discussed every area of our future lives together: money,
sex, family background, upbringing, career, spirituality, raising children, everything you can imagine. We left nothing to
chance, and at the end we had a lot of practical information
that told us we were extremely compatible as husband and
wife.

The sessions also brought some difficult things to light.
That was another way in which that time was so valuable.

MEAGAN: Some damage from my previous relationships became clear in counseling, but one of the most memorable issues came up during a session with the counselor where we talked about my smoking. I said I wanted to quit smoking, and while I wasn't sure how far off that was, I definitely wanted to do it. Then she asked DeVon what he thought about it, and he matter-of-factly said, "I'm not going to marry a smoker."

I was shocked, because this was our pre-marriage counseling. One of the reasons I had picked up smoking was that I had a difficult time transitioning from child actor to adult actor; I was dealing with harsh amounts of criticism and judgment. The Internet was just starting to become a thing, and I constantly felt exposed to opinions and judgment. I became self-destructive out of anger and pain. When I got past that stage, the only thing left was smoking cigarettes. Smoking was me flipping the bird to everyone. I kept smoking over the many times I tried to quit because people were always trying to force me to quit. Because of those years of growing up as a child actor, I despise anyone trying to manipulate my direction. I had an infantile reaction to it.

When DeVon said he didn't want to marry a smoker, it felt like another blow, another judgment—another assessment of me not being good enough. I couldn't focus on the rest of the session. We went to dinner and I couldn't speak. I was low-key devastated. It was as if he had said I was not good enough to marry as I was at that moment.

DEVON: That comment was a reflex. She was trying to quit, and I was saying that from the standpoint of wanting her to quit before we got married. I had no idea how it would affect her. I think that when you get close to the finish line, you start thinking about the things that aren't exactly as you want them to be, and you start trying to force them to get there, which doesn't work. You can't marry someone with the idea of changing them.

The desire for Meagan to quit smoking came from the fact that I love her deeply and want her around for a hundred years. But I didn't state that desire in a healthy way at that point.

MEAGAN: We talked about it, he apologized, and in our marriage vows he actually said, "Even if you never change, I will love you exactly the way that you are." That was the single most powerful thing anyone could ever have said to me. No one had ever said that to me before, that they accepted me for me, without condition.

All I wanted was to be accepted for myself (flaws and all). I knew I was and will always be a work in progress, but I accepted myself as such, and I needed DeVon to accept me also. His acceptance of me gave me the courage, freedom, and desire to quit smoking. I struggled before because the desire mainly came from wanting to quit as a way to please someone else. This time I wanted to quit for myself because I loved someone who accepted me and I want to be around for both of us.

DEVON: My wish for her to quit smoking never went away, but my ability to handle it and have patience with it and love her and have a vibrant marriage has only grown. According to Meagan and my family (and I guess I'd have to agree) I've loosened up and become a lot less rigid and unyielding. By creating a safe, nonjudgmental environment as her husband, I helped give her the strength to say on her own, "I need to move past this."

When we tell others about our data-driven premarital counseling, we get polarized responses. Some people think it was very wise. Others think we sucked the romance out of our romance. This is exactly the myth we want to dispel. Marriage should not be about deliberately courting surprises. You're not going on a vacation where you can say, "Honey, let's take that road and see where we end up." You're selecting a person with whom you might spend the rest of your life, with whom you might have children. Life and marriage throw enough surprises at you, so why would you want to leave anything to chance when you're choosing the partner who will be by your side? What's romantic about not fully knowing the person you're marrying?

The time to learn everything you can about how compatible you two are in every area of your lives comes before you're engaged. It's the time to bring buried issues—like the smoking thing—into the light so you can discuss, understand, and resolve them.

This is an exciting but potentially perilous time. You've found someone you think you want to spend your life with— your God-ordained wife or husband. That's exciting. You're talking about getting engaged, getting married, or maybe even planning a wedding. It can be tempting to surrender any reservations you might have and just roll with it. Don't. This is the most critical part of The Wait, when you can have faith but shouldn't abandon reason. You need both.

It's fun to be starry-eyed and in love. But then you start saying things like, "It's meant to be" and "It doesn't matter, this is true love." You start pretending, glossing over differences, and ignoring things that really matter. That's a danger zone. While it's true that when you find the person God intends for you, it really is meant to be, how can you be sure the person you've committed to is that person without learning more? Wait and don't turn off your rational mind.

LIVE AS YOU BEFORE YOU LIVE AS WE

One of the most common regrets among couples who got married too soon is that they didn't get to live their lives as singles while they had the chance. That's sad, because there's nothing stopping you from living the life you want—the life that God wants you to live so you can learn all about yourself. If you wait, you avoid entanglements that can tie you down at a time when you could be having adventures, seeing the world, and discovering what it's like to live in different places, try different jobs, and date different people.

These are some of the experiences we think worth sampling while you're young and unencumbered:

- Travel. If you do nothing else, see as much of God's world as you can. It's a wondrous, thrilling place that will take you out of your comfort zone and show you new sides of yourself.
- Serve. God calls us to serve others and give of our spirits, and there's no better time to do this than when you're single. Try many ways of serving until you find one that moves you: feeding the homeless, reading to children in hospitals, building homes for Habitat for Humanity, and so on.
- Work for yourself. Not everyone is cut out for self-employment, but if you've always wanted to see if you could make a living doing your own business, there's no time like the present.

- Pursue your passion. Whether your passion is music, dance, writing, acting, or art, it's part of you. Making a career out of that passion, however, takes a lot of work and sacrifice, and those are much easier to endure when you're not asking a significant other to endure them with you.

- Relocate. Always wanted to live in New York or Los Angeles? Go for it! That's a lot harder to do when you're with someone else.

IF YOU'RE READY, DON'T BE AFRAID TO MOVE AHEAD

When you're committing to each other because your love is deep and mature and based on really *knowing* each other, it's right. But then don't mess around. When our relationship began, we weren't looking for another boyfriend-girlfriend thing where we spent years in limbo, not really knowing what was happening. It's normal and healthy *not* to want to be someone's significant other for another two, three, or four years, because all too often that results in wasted time and a lot of baggage. We had both been there, done that.

In other words, we were ready to become committed. *Commitment* can have a lot of meanings, but for The Wait it has only one: marriage. Make no mistake: all roads lead to marriage. Practicing The Wait, celibacy, dating—it's all part of a journey intended to lead to marriage to the person God intends you to be with.

We understand that there are a lot of unhealthy views of marriage. Plenty of people expect marriage to complete them. They treat it like some magical state that will change them as soon as they say "I do." This actually isn't true. Saying "I do" is the beginning, not the end.

You're saying, "I choose you."

In our culture, many people are starting to see marriage as old-fashioned. Young people are less likely to marry, and if they do marry, they're waiting longer. That's smart, because the older you get, the more you learn about yourself and what you want.

If you love someone but dating exclusively is as far as you're willing to go, what you're saying is, "I think you're right for me, but I'm not sure." That's fine for a while, because we all need time to get to know one another. But when that sort of situation goes on and on for years, one or both partners are dodging true commitment.

Maybe they're comfortable with what they have but fear marriage for reasons of their own. Maybe they're not sure the other person is the One and are afraid to wreck a good thing by being honest. People duck marriage for all sorts of reasons, from not wanting to be tied down to not wanting children.

We have a friend who's a very successful Hollywood

screenwriter. A few years back, he fell head over heels for a woman and relocated back East with her. For three years they became intertwined in each other's lives—becoming part of each other's families, the whole Hallmark picture. Except . . . they never moved toward marriage. Eventually, our friend confronted her about getting married, and she told him she wasn't sure if she wanted to. After waiting another year to see if things would change, he conceded that she just wasn't sure that he was the One. They broke up and he had to pick up the pieces. (Which ultimately led him to the real person he was supposed to be with, and he's happier now than ever before.)

There's a clear line between The Wait and waiting around. If you're just waiting around, you're doing it out of indecision, fear, or laziness. If you and your partner are communicating, sharing, being honest, exploring new things together, and keeping your objectivity, you shouldn't need more than a year to figure out whether God intended you for each other. If you're stuck in one of those stages for much longer, start asking why.

MEAGAN: Our relationship was the first that I didn't want to be someone's girlfriend again. I was tired of that. I was ready to find my life partner. I didn't want to get too comfortable, either. I wasn't ready to spend too much time in a dating relationship with a person I already knew I was going to marry. When you know the qualities and morals of a person, share the same desires, get along with him, and enjoy him enough as a human being in such a way that you can see weathering any storm together and being happy, then it's time.

DEVON: I was looking for clarity, so when Meagan said she didn't want to "be a girlfriend" I thought, "What does that mean? What's our understanding? Does that mean she's okay with us dating others?" I didn't want to see anyone else, which was good because I found out that she didn't, either. She simply didn't want to waste her time in a dating relationship that had no future, and I respected that. So we were committed early on. Now, I needed and wanted the boyfriend-girlfriend label because it gave me clarity. It was important to me as a man. If you don't have clear parameters, you can veer off into other things—other women. So I took the initiative to not date anybody else, and I shut down anybody who expressed an interest in dating me. That made it clear to both of us: we are committed.

Cleaning up your dating life is an important part of getting ready for commitment. This might include doing things like cutting ties to exes you still hang out with or being honest about being with someone you're starting to like instead of hiding it. Doing this says to the person you're dating, "I'm ready to take the next step toward seeing if you are the one God has in mind for me." But keep moving forward. If you and the person you're dating have spent many months or even years together, but you've stopped asking important questions and learning more about each other, then you may be in that maddening limbo that does nobody any good. Staying there will only lead to heartbreak.

BREAKING THE STALEMATE

Then we have the other kind of waiting, when neither partner can seem to commit to an exclusive relationship. You have a stalemate, a catch-22 situation where both people are waiting on the other to commit before committing themselves. Sometimes this happens because one or both people have been hurt and are overcautious; other times, it's because of irrational fears about cutting off other options or some such nonsense that translates to "I'm still hoping to meet someone hotter/younger/richer/more compliant than you." In any case, if stalemates don't end quickly, they don't end well. Inevitably, one person gets impatient and moves on.

Like so much else, the solution can be found in communication and faith. If you're dating, you should be communicating. With a few honest, inquisitive conversations, it's really not that hard to figure out if someone you're dating is serious or not. If he or she isn't that person, then the pressure's off! You can keep dating for enjoyment, or you can choose to move on to other people. But don't allow your relationship to be one of assumption:

"I assume she's ready for commitment."

"I assume she wants children."

"I assume he wants to get married someday."

Don't assume. Ask. And if you don't get clear answers, ask again. Assumptions can set you up for massive disappointment.

REASONS NOT TO COMMIT

There are plenty of good reasons to just say no to commitment. Sometimes we're looking for love but we're not ready for it emotionally. There's still some work we need to do on ourselves, some personal heavy lifting that demands focus and concentration and sacrifice for a while longer.

Reluctance to commit often comes from a deep knowing that it's not time, despite all the signals that it is. Committing before you're ready is worse than not committing at all. The person you're aching for? If they're who God has set up for you, they'll be there when you're ready, despite all the obstacles that might come between you.

Another reason to hesitate is because you realize you've chosen a person because she or he was willing to wait—and not much else. Someone trusting you enough to give up sex for you is a wonderful thing, but you can't build a relationship on that alone. Once The Wait is over, you still need someone with whom you're compatible in every way, and compatibility goes far beyond the desire to abstain from sex.

You shouldn't commit because of pressure or fear that you're falling behind, either. The pursuit of true love is one of patience. You can't succumb to the pressure to rush into a relationship or into marriage because everybody else is doing it. The people who pressure us into marriage are often the same ones who ask, "Why didn't it work out?" Let yourself be pushed into a commitment too soon, and you might find yourself stuck in something you weren't ready for.

DEVON: I was the last one of my brothers to get married. So many times, I would get grief from my family for not being married. They would say, "DeVon, you're just too caught up in the industry," or, "DeVon, you're too hard to please." But I knew what love needed to feel like and

I needed to know the person God was bringing me was in love with him first. So I wasn't going to compromise. I wasn't going to give in to the pressure to get married before I knew I was ready, no matter how many times people asked me when I was going to settle down.

You also should never commit because it's what someone else wants. Whenever you make a decision motivated by pleasing someone else because you don't want to disappoint or upset them, you will *always* make the wrong decision.

DEVON: Here's a story about that idea that I'll never forget. When I was in seventh grade, I had a crush on a girl. She was the apple of my eye. But while Tamica wasn't thinking about me, her best friend, Nikki, sure was. She had a huge crush on me, but I only had eyes for Tamica. Classic middle-school love triangle. One day, Nikki got up the nerve to ask me if I would be her boyfriend. I didn't want to, but because I knew that if I said yes it would make Tamica happy, I told Nikki I would. She was elated and ran around the entire school telling everybody that we were going steady. My plan worked; it made Tamica happy.

However, as soon as I got home from school, I broke out in a cold sweat, because I knew I didn't like Nikki enough to be her boyfriend. I was racked with anxiety.

The next day, I wrote Nikki a note and told her I had made a mistake. I broke up with her and didn't even have enough courage to tell her to her face. She was devastated and started crying. Later that day, Tamica came up to me and said, "If you didn't like her, you shouldn't have said yes," and walked away. Not only did I break Nikki's heart, but I messed things up with Tamica, too.

There's no shame in going a distance down the road with someone only to decide that long-term commitment isn't best. It's much better than making a false commitment because you fear being alone or making the other person upset. But do it quickly and honestly. It may be painful, but eventually you'll both realize that it was for the best.

LEARNING . . . EVERY DATE, EVERY DAY

But let's say that things are great and you are both ready to commit for all the right reasons. You'll discover that a committed relationship is a master class on human nature. Spending much of your time with one person and sharing the most intimate details of your lives quickly shatters romantic delusions and childish ideas about love at first sight and happily ever after.

Happily ever after does happen, but not every day . . . or even every hour. There are ups and downs, fights and reconciliations, crises and doubts. The mark of a deep, mature, and unbreakable bond is the ability to weather those storms—to respect, admire, appreciate, and love each other even when you disagree, when you're not at your most attractive, or when your schedules are so busy that intimate time is a distant memory. Your goal is to fall in love not with the body, face, clothes, or title but the person—the spirit—underneath. That's who you'll still love madly in fifty years.

For this reason, learning and communicating assume their most vital roles in this part of The Wait.

Ask yourself "why?" about everything.

If this seems like we're asking you to audition your partner for a role . . . well, that's exactly what we're doing. This is serious business! We're talking about your potential life partner in all things. At this stage, to wait is to watch out for your interests, becoming as sure as possible that this is the husband or wife God has in mind for you. You'll do that only if you keep your head and look at the things he or she does with a critical eye—without being critical of them, of course.

Remember, what's normal for you is not necessarily normal to your partner. What you regard as a virtue, he or she may see as a flaw. You're going to discover things about this person over time that, no matter how well you thought you knew them, will throw you. Now's the time to learn how you'll react to those surprises so that when they come later you can respond not with judgment but compassion, clarity, and love.

There are a lot of ways to do this. Though it might seem clinical and unromantic, we highly recommend the kind of four-month assessment and counseling process we went through. Having all those facts on the table and a professional counselor to help us sort through them really put us on a firm footing. We discovered that while drama and volatility might seem romantic, compatibility and deep knowledge of each other are what great relationships are really made of.

You might also consider:

- Spiritual counseling. Talking with your minster or lay spiritual counselor about your beliefs, relationship with God, and other issues can be very revealing without being as rigorous or potentially off-putting as a long questionnaire.
- Regular Q&A sessions. We don't want to turn your dating life into *Shark Tank,* but it wouldn't hurt to schedule one night every week or two where you two sit down and talk about a specific topic that's relevant to your future: goals, children, lifestyle, parents, mutual

interests, and so on. Set whatever ground rules suit you and then stick to them.

- Travel. Traveling together is the classic test of a relationship's health. You're under stress, sharing common space, often with different expectations.

Find your own way, but find a way. Remember, just because you want to commit to this person doesn't mean they're the person God intends for you to be with. Take your time to figure that out.

SHOULD YOU LIVE LIKE YOU'RE MARRIED WHEN YOU'RE NOT?

Once people think they're with the person God wants them to marry, they often take the next step: move in together. However, while plenty of men and women have lived together and had successful marriages (including a few couples in our own families), it's not our recommendation. We know this isn't a popular stance to take in today's relationship culture; however, we can only speak from our experience and what has worked for us.

Living together wasn't even on the table for us; we didn't move in together until after our wedding. We saw that God was setting us up for something incredible, and we wanted to take the time to really get to know each other without the pressure of pretending we were already husband and wife.

It's essential not to avoid acting like you're married before you actually are. Doing that establishes expectations that can become impossible to live up to. We have a good friend who's been with his girlfriend for five or six years, living together for much of that time. They're trying to do The Wait, but it's tough when you're sharing the same space. Celibacy is extremely difficult, and you start playacting the part of the married couple: cooking meals, sharing the shopping, hosting holiday parties, and all the rest.

The thing is, you're not married. So cohabitation is another form of limbo where one or both of you can easily start presuming that you should be treated like a spouse even though you're not. Marriage is a formal, powerful commitment: "I choose you and no one else." Until you and your partner have made that commitment, you could still be eyeing the exits when tempers flare, schedules conflict, or a big argument erupts.

There's a time to act like husband and wife, but it doesn't come until you're actually married—until you have that indelible commitment to each other. Acting married when you're not can set you up for heartbreak. If someone's not committing to you permanently, it's usually for a reason. They aren't sure. They aren't ready. There's nothing wrong with that;

however, they should take the time to get sure and ready! But that may not be as likely to happen if you're living together.

MEAGAN: My last boyfriend before DeVon lived in Florida, so while I didn't live with him, I was there about 70 percent of the time. That proved damaging because his space wasn't my space, and I always felt like it wasn't my space. As much as I felt like the woman of the house, it wasn't mine. I was just there. My life wasn't there. When something would go wrong, I would expect special treatment because I was the lady of the house, but I wouldn't get it. I felt completely betrayed. So I rebelled: not cooking for anybody, not cleaning, not doing anything.

When I felt shortchanged or I expected something that he wasn't going to provide, we would argue violently—and the way we argued was completely out of my comfort zone, that's not who I was or wanted to be. Living together under those circumstances made me act like someone other than who I am because I was playing a role! It's the same for anyone. You're not yourself when you're living with implications and expectations that just aren't supported by reality.

DEVON: That experience damaged Meagan in ways that we're still dealing with. She put herself in a situation where the man was not ready to commit at the level that she was already committed. Even today, if she feels slighted in that way, or if anything in our marriage evokes the same negative experience, she'll react defensively, angrily. Those echoes haven't faded yet.

It was different for me. My younger and older brothers were married before me. My cousin and best friend were married before me. I didn't want to rush into a lifelong commitment just because everybody else was doing it. I was not yet ready. Before Meagan, I was in a significant relationship with a young lady who had been a friend. She was everything on the List. We'd been together for a year, and everyone assumed we would get married. But I just wasn't ready, and I had to break it off. It was very painful. But the pain would have been much greater if I'd lied to myself.

Lots of couples live together thinking it's the logical next step before marriage, but that decision may actually move you farther away from getting married. You're already acting like you're married, so why bother with the formality?

THE FRIENDS-AND-FAMILY PLAN

We'd be remiss if we didn't take a moment to talk about the impact that friends and family can have on a couple's commitment. When you get serious about someone, you're excited to tell your friends and family members all about it. They're just as excited, firing endless questions and speculating about whether you'll get married, have kids, the whole thing. We've both had relationships where our significant others became as intertwined with our families as they did with us. But not knowing how to manage friends and family can make it harder to handle commitment with objectivity and restraint.

In relationships, friends and family members tend to fall into two camps: defenders and advocates. Defenders are skeptical, even cynical, about the person you're dating. Is he good enough for you? Has he unfriended his ex-girlfriends? Why not? They're looking out for your interests, and while they can prompt you to ask some good questions, they can easily cross over into the negative, finding fault where there isn't any.

Advocates are absolutely uncritical about the person you're with, even when they should be. As soon as you tell them all about the person you're with, they want to know where the ring will come from and when you'll pop the question. They're so pumped that you're in a relationship that they could push you to move faster than you're comfortable going. Obviously, this is potentially a problem. Being in The Wait is about being patient and letting things develop in their own time. When you let well-meaning family members or close friends push you out of your comfort zone, you sabotage yourself.

However, if you manage friends and family right, they can be assets to your journey as a couple, even before you get together.

DEVON: I'm blessed with some amazing, strong women in my life—my mother and my aunts. They and many of my other family members have weighed in on my dating life and even forewarned me that I would defy my own intentions and marry someone in the entertainment business. That was clearly a sign from God, and I paid attention, which I think kept me more open-minded about Meagan than I might have been if I'd only been thinking about my List. When she met my mother and aunts, they immediately took to her and saw something really special in her. I'm sure that was one more push that helped bring us together.

MEAGAN: During those nine months prior to dating DeVon, when I told many of my friends that God had told me DeVon was my husband, more than a few of them looked at me like I was a little crazy. That was a good test of my faith. The ones who took me seriously were valuable sources of information about his celibacy and his role as a minister. I learned a lot about this man while I was still in a place of waiting that I never would have learned without those friends.

Managing the "help" of family and friends is simple. Just wait. If you don't want them intruding into your dating life, then wait to tell them about the one you like until you're sure that you're ready to pursue a deeper relationship.

PASSION CHEMISTRY

Even if you're practicing The Wait and remaining celibate, you need to assess if you and the person you're dating have passion chemistry. This is very important. Just because you practice The Wait doesn't guarantee you're going to have a great sex life when you get married.

A great sex life has a lot to do with the chemistry you have with the person you're getting serious with. Is there a passion between you? Desire that goes beyond the strictly physical? How intense does it get when you kiss? It's important to monitor this (obviously within the confines of still practicing The Wait) because it matters. Marriage doesn't automatically light a stove where the pilot light was out. So don't be afraid to kiss each other or hold each other, because if there isn't passion chemistry, this is a red flag that you'll need to address (through counseling, books, or pastoral help) if you want to have a strong and healthy marriage.

POPPING THE QUESTION

You've asked the good questions and received good answers. You've revealed your scars and darker side and seen your partner's, and it's cool. You've come to know each other's character and heart. You're ready. Ready to make the ultimate commitment of marriage. Good.

God brought you together to forsake all others and to help each other become the people He created you to be, and marriage is the surest way to make that happen. So when you're sure, get engaged. But be engaged only as long as it takes to plan your wedding. We're not believers in long engagements. Some people use the engagement as another phase of testing compatibility, but that's another way of saying, "I'm not sure." If you're not sure, don't get engaged!

Men in particular are more likely to ask, "Will you marry me?" as a holding action, because they don't want to lose the woman they're with. Then they insist on a two-year engagement to buy more time to figure out what they want. Get engaged because you really are serious about getting married, not because you need another excuse *not* to get married. You owe each other better than that.

When a couple is really ready and the proposal is confident and sincere, it can be magic. That's what happened to us.

DEVON: Meagan had thought I was going to propose around New Year's. Her family was even asking, "So, did anything interesting happen on New Year's Eve?" I knew that I was ready to marry her because I had enough time to consider what was out there and to evaluate what her life would add to mine. But I wasn't ready to propose just then. Then in February of 2012 I ordered the ring.

In March, Meagan came by my office on the same day I'd had the ring delivered there. But I wasn't going to do it there. That weekend, she was leaving to go to New York to shoot the pilot for the TV series *Deception*. Still unsure of what to do, I called my younger brother and said, "I think I'm supposed to propose today but I don't know. I'm looking for a sign." He started praying on it. When I got to her house, she had thrown on a shirt that one of my mother's friends had gotten my brothers and me. It read, "Got Franklin?" I stopped her on the balcony, took a picture of her in the shirt, and sent it to my brother. He said, "That's crazy!"

Then we went to eat at this Jamaican restaurant. At the end of *Jumping the Broom* (the film where we first got to know each other) is a song called "Cupid Shuffle." Guess what song came on the sound system at the restaurant? I had my sign.

We went back home and started watching TV, and

then she had to get ready to go to the airport. Suddenly, I was incredibly nervous. I knew I had to do this now.

MEAGAN: I was lying on his chest, and all of a sudden I heard "Boom! Boom!" His heart was pounding. I said, "Are you okay?" He said he was nervous because I was leaving town, and he was making his way over to the closet while giving me this fishy line about me being out of town for a long time . . . and then he brings this wooden box out of his jacket pocket. I was trying to figure out what it was, and when I finally figured it out, I was like, "Oh my God, oh my God."

I heard some of what he said about him and me, but mostly I was freaking out. Then he came over and got on one knee. Of course I said yes. Then I was jumping on the bed like a little kid, but there was no time to celebrate, because we had to jam to LAX. We called my sister from the car and she alternated between speaking and screaming from excitement.

Planning our wedding was easy. We decided to get married in June, and none of it felt a moment too soon. We didn't disagree on anything. "Do you like this?" "Yes." "Do you want that?" "Yes." No drama. No stress. We were two people who were finally exactly where we needed to be, and with whom we needed to be with.

MARRIAGE AND BEYOND

Of course, getting married is easy. Being married is hard. There's a lot to sort out: gender roles, living together, and combining households, for starters. But if you reach your wedding in the right way, while waiting and continuing to learn about each other, you should be strong and solid at this point. That's not to say there aren't challenges; we still face them. Each of us does things the other doesn't like, from leaving clothes on the floor (DeVon) to leaving stacks of miscellaneous papers next to the bed (Meagan).

We've had to figure out who's responsible for taking out the trash and making meals. We have to flex and chill when one of us is coming off a long location shoot or a long day of development meetings followed by a premiere. But those things are minor compared to all we've been through to find and really understand each other.

Marriage may be the finish line for celibacy, but the need for sexual discipline doesn't end after you exchange rings. It's dangerous to use sex to wallpaper over conflicts and differences that call for honest communication. The simple solution for that: never have important discussions in bed. It's much too easy to become . . . pleasantly distracted.

One of the questions we field often is "When are you having children?" There's little doubt that we'd like to have children one day, but not now. The biggest thing for us is living for our marriage, giving ourselves all the tools we need to be the best we can be. Right now we're about learning all we can, growing together, and having a solid platform for working God's will.

Having children changes everything. If you both want them right away, then have them. If not, then don't bow to pressure from anyone. Give yourselves time to be married. The time before children is a special window for just the two of you. Children are another reason to wait—to ask questions, communicate, and watch for signs from God. The worst thing you can do is make babies because someone's mom wants grandchildren.

You've seen the marriages: a couple has kids before they're ready, and they never get to live their lives. Then the moment the kids leave for college, the marriage is over. Apart from the children, they had nothing keeping them together. Not only didn't they know each other, they didn't even like each other. That's a waste.

You're a parent for a lifetime. You'll never get that pre-parenting time back. You can stay up late, travel, go to the movies, and live with total freedom. Raising children is a joy, but so is knowing that you're really, really ready before you make that leap.

THE BLESSINGS OF MARRIAGE

You really can have the life you and your spouse want if you wait on things to happen when you and God are ready. Life is better when you have patience and let the Lord work, because you allow him to bring you the right person at the time He knows is right. Neither of us was expecting to date each other and marry so quickly, and there have been challenges, but we trusted God and it's been incredible. We've grown. Doors have opened, allowing us to travel the world and talk about marriage and sex and relationships. Our careers have gone in new directions because of our marriage. We've been able to help people.

In part, we probably came through so well because we were older, in our thirties, with a lot of life experience behind us. It's important to come into a marriage already knowing who you are and not counting on your marriage to change or complete you. Marriage will change you, but not in the ways you expect. You should be complete before committing to someone who's going to complement you.

We can both look back with confidence that we lived single lives without regret before we got married. We know we're never going to reflect and say with regret, "I wish I had done that before I got married." We did "that." We built incredible careers. We've seen the world. We've done amazing things on our own, and now we'll do them together.

Waiting to commit to a relationship until you have life experience is a smart move. It helps you understand who you want to be. It helps you understand the purpose that God has in mind for you.

Some other advice we'd like to leave you with:

- Don't base your marriage on preconceived ideals. Let your marriage find its rhythm. Every marriage is a unique organism; it's important to give that organism time to live, evolve, and settle into what it's going to be.
- Don't expect your partner to change because you're married. You can't change someone else in marriage, but marriage will change you.
- Have a clear sense of your own identity before you marry. If you don't know who you are before you get married, marriage will not teach you. Instead, you'll become a person's wife and then someone's mom. You'll lose yourself. Understand who you are as a union, but also understand who you are independent of the union.

Whatever road you take, we wish you a marriage that's as joyous and blessed as ours has been.

CHAPTER NINE

DON'T GIVE UP

We must be willing to get rid of the life we've planned,
so as to have the life that is waiting for us.
—JOSEPH CAMPBELL

There's a woman we know who, until she was in her midthirties, spun her wheels in painful relationship after painful relationship. She was a classic savior, a woman who always tried to fix men who were troubled or bad boys. But when she got into a serious relationship, she spent so much energy taking care of the man's needs that she never stood up for what she wanted. Inevitably, her boyfriends would lose respect for her and end up breaking up with her. For years, she repeated this pattern again and again and wondered why things never changed.

Then finally, after yet another brutal breakup, she stopped to pray and heard a voice asking, "If you stand up for what you want, what's the worst that could happen?" It was a revelation. She finally saw her pattern of behavior clearly and realized that the one common factor in all her failed relationships was her.

From that point on, she vowed to change things. She went into a time of waiting. She became celibate. She cleaned up her social relationships. She pursued several long-standing goals and spent some therapeutic time alone, journaling and praying. And she discovered that she had the courage to put her own needs first in a relationship—that she was worthy. A few months later, she met an incredible man who, as it turned out, lived on the same street. But she hadn't been able to "see" him until she was ready in mind and spirit. Eventually, they became husband and wife.

If you have been celibate for a time and still have not met your spouse, you may find yourself saying, "I've been waiting but nothing's happening. I'm getting tired and discouraged. What do I now?" The frustration is understandable. People are giving up sex, which is tough enough. On top of that, you might be taking a break from dating, spending more time alone, and confronting your darkest relationship demons. Despite all this, you still haven't met the person God means for you to be with. Maybe you've been practicing The Wait—or at least, you think you've been practicing it—but you're not getting what you want yet.

We thought we'd close this book by addressing this distressing situation.

THE WAIT ALWAYS WORKS

First, let's get one thing out of the way right now: The Wait always produces results. We've made it clear that The Wait is about more than giving up sex. It's more than sitting around not doing anything. Still, there are a lot of people who are simply waiting around for good things to happen and wasting their precious time.

By our best estimate, based on the stories we hear from friends and colleagues, many of those frustrated individuals are women. We have heard from and spoken with many women who are frustrated that they have spent years abstaining from sex in order to let that one godly man come into their lives. Still, nothing. They're angry, confused, and near panic. If you're in this position, you may be wondering if The Wait is real, if you've done something wrong, or if you should just marry the first eligible person you can find before you spend the rest of your life alone. We have some suggestions that we hope will provide clarity and give you some peace.

BEWARE OF PITFALLS

How you wait is as important as why. We want you to enjoy the kind of life bliss that we have been so blessed to find, so let's get to work. If you have been patiently hoping for better days in your romantic life but aren't seeing them yet, here are some possible reasons why your wait could be setting you back rather than helping you:

You're waiting for a certain person. Is there a certain man or woman you've always had your eye on? Do you believe that if you practice The Wait, God will align your paths and bring you together? Unfortunately, it doesn't necessarily work that way. It's possible that the object of your affection is the one you're intended to be with but it's even more probable that he or she might not be. Our story is a perfect example of that: we weren't even on each other's dating radar for years before the Lord started bringing us together. Don't be so fixated on a certain person that you pray for them instead of praying for God's will. Because if you can only see God answering your prayer if He brings you the person you have your eye on, you might pass right by his ideal match for you.

You're waiting for God to do all the work. The Wait is a two-way street. God does some of the work, but you have to do your share. You can't just stop having sex, then sit at home nursing the same grudges and compulsions and wounds and say, "Okay, Lord, I'm ready for you to bring me my spouse!" We've said that when and how God brings you your partner is as important as *who* He brings, and this is what we mean. Imagine if that person came into your life when nothing had changed. Would you recognize him or her? Would your old bad habits sabotage the relationship before it even got started?

The Wait operates on a straightforward premise: you put in the work to become your best self, and God will put you into your best life.

You don't really know why you're waiting. Certainly there comes a time in everyone's dating life where they're tempted to throw up their hands, swear off the opposite sex forever, and retreat into the house with Apple TV and the number of a local pizza-delivery place. That's understandable. But most of us get our groove back after a weekend of moping and head back out to try again. If you haven't, and you're just on indefinite hold from relationships in the hopes that something good will happen, you're probably going to wind up even more frustrated.

PLENTY TO DO IN THE MEANTIME

The Wait is just as much about self-improvement through delayed gratification as it is about love. The clearer you are about how you want to better yourself while you're waiting, the more successful you will be. As we've mentioned before, these are some of the important areas we suggest you focus on if you're planning your own time of waiting:

- Health and fitness
- Personal finance (paying off debts, buying a house, investing for retirement)
- Career
- Education
- Travel
- Entrepreneurship (starting a business, working for a start-up)
- Spirituality (going to church more regularly, honing your openness to the Word, becoming adept at prayer, learning to read God's signs and portents)
- Creativity (painting, acting, composing music, writing a novel, doing standup comedy)
- Helping others, doing charitable work, etc.

TRUST WHAT YOU CAN'T SEE

The Wait, like any other practice, takes, well, practice. It's a skill and a discipline, and your experience might not be smooth and even throughout your time of waiting. You might start off feeling isolated and sexually frustrated, only to feel the wind at your back as soon as you start a class or talk to your minister. You may go along for months feeling like you're exactly where you need to be, only to run into an old flame at the grocery store and spend the weekend in a depressed funk. Like any discipline, The Wait has its ups and downs, its periods of achievement, and it plateaus when it seems like nothing is happening.

But here's the thing: even when it seems like nothing is happening, if you're executing The Wait faithfully and doing the work, good things are happening. You just might not be able to see them yet. Much of God's work happens behind the scenes where it's not obvious to our perceptions. Faith keeps us going through those quiet times, trusting that if we persist and stay true to our intention, He will reward us.

It's a little like sending the manuscript of your novel to a publisher. You do your best work, cast it into the universe, and cross your fingers. Then you wait. The book might sit on an editor's desk for months before he reads it, but when he does, he loves it and sends you a letter telling you that he wants to publish it (yes, they still send letters; publishing is an old-fashioned business). All this time, while your manuscript is waiting to be read and while the congratulatory letter is making its way to your door, you're unaware that something terrific is on its way. Your only recourse is faith. Then one day, the letter arrives and your faith is rewarded.

STAY ON GOD'S TIMETABLE

There's just one problem: as far as you know, you've been practicing The Wait just as we've suggested. You're doing it for the right reasons, doing the work on your mind and character, and staying disciplined about sex. But nothing has happened, and you're starting to lose hope that it ever will. What are you doing wrong?

First of all, you might not be doing anything wrong. You may just not have practiced The Wait for enough time. The biggest leap of faith involved in The Wait lies in not knowing how long it's going to take for your husband or wife to become apparent to you. It could be six months. It could be six years. It will happen when you are mentally, emotionally, and spiritually ready, but there's no way to know when that will be.

There's also no reliable way to speed things up. Seek counseling, go back to church, clean up your diet—those are all beneficial things, but none of them will move up your timetable if God doesn't will it. You don't know when that time is going to come; there could be a crisis on your horizon that will propel you into a new way of thinking. Maybe someone new, who's not your husband or wife, will come into your life to be the bridge to the person who is.

In this case, it's difficult for us to say, "Just keep waiting," but that's what we have to do. You must have faith that God will make your wait worthwhile. What if that meeting with your future spouse is right around the corner, but you sabotage it after years of discipline by giving up and going to back to your old ways? That would be tragic. Besides, waiting can benefit you in many more ways than bringing you and your meant-to-be partner together. For example, during your wait have you:

- Experienced less drama and more stable friendships?
- Dated some really interesting people?
- Gotten to know yourself at a deeper level?
- Let go of past emotional baggage?
- Broken self-destructive behavior patterns?
- Gotten physically fit and mentally healthier?
- Advanced your career?
- Pursued your dreams?
- Become more deeply spiritual and drawn closer to God?

If the answer to any of these questions is yes, you've profited from The Wait. This practice may be a matter of finding the person with whom God wants you to do great things, but its core is about personal evolution. It's about being at peace with who you were, who you are, and who you're becoming. If you spend five years waiting and achieve that, can you honestly call the time wasted even if it takes longer to meet your spouse? We don't believe so.

THE WAIT AND . . . SELF-ESTEEM

Self-esteem is the eight-hundred-pound gorilla in the room, the reason so many of us go astray before discovering The Wait. God may love us, we know, but we don't always love ourselves very much. So many of the problems that we bring upon ourselves, from addiction to remaining in damaging and even abusive relationships, stem from the deep-down belief that we can't do better, don't deserve better.

The Wait comes into play here because rather than confront the reasons why we harbor such feelings of worthlessness and self-hatred, we often run from them by pursuing instant gratification. Serial dating, casual sex, drinking, getting wrapped up in other people's dramas—they're often ways to avoid dealing with our own pain. But pain doesn't just heal without attention. It waits beneath the surface and poisons everything in our lives.

The solution is to reject the quick fix of a drink or a one-nighter that temporarily dulls the pain. Face the reasons why you're in pain. It's hard and it's something you shouldn't do alone, but it's definitely something you should do. There is life on the other side of trauma, self-loathing, and bitterness, and it can be amazing. The first step is being willing to stare down your pain and not look away. Do that and you can do the rest.

REFLECT AND REVIEW

Another reason that you might not have found your spouse is that, to be perfectly honest, you already did. But you didn't recognize the person as your spouse when he or she was in front of you, and the opportunity passed you by. Don't panic. If that is what happened, it isn't the end of the world. There are several possibilities at work. You may not have been at a place in your development where you could "see" that person as special. Maybe he or she didn't conform to your List, and you said, "Pass."

If that happened, don't lose hope. If you recall, the two of us orbited each other for four years before we finally started dating. If God means for you to be with someone, He will bring you together though the obstacles seem insurmountable.

Another possibility—one we spoke about early on—is that you became a different person through your practice of The Wait, and God decided that the person He originally had in mind for you was not your ideal partner after all. Free will gives us each the power to choose our own emotional, intellectual, and spiritual path. If that path curves unexpectedly, the person we thought was right for us may become just another date. In that case, your continued wait may just be a matter of God aligning your path with the new man or woman who will help you become the best version of yourself.

If that's not the reason behind your frustration, then it's possible that despite starting The Wait with the best of intentions, you've fallen into a rut. You're not pushing yourself to grow and learn like you used to, and this has slowed your progress to a crawl. This is more common with long wait periods, because boredom and complacency naturally set in. If you're not seeing electric results from your dating and you've reached your immediate personal goals, it's easy to get too comfortable. Before you know it—*clunk*—you've fallen into a rut that's not much more effective than your previous pattern of behavior.

Some people think the best defense against this sort of thing is discipline, but that will take you only so far. A long wait is a little like training for a triathlon: you're putting in a lot of work over a very long period of time for a reward that may come sometime in the future, but the work itself can become an obsession that blocks blessings. Discipline is good, but we think it's better to have people in your life who will hold you accountable.

We do that for each other. Friends, family members, your minister, mentors—any of them can be your accountability check-ins. Tell them about The Wait, what you're doing and why, and what your goal is. Ask them to say something if they see you getting too comfortable or not moving forward in your life.

A final reason that The Wait may not be yielding results

for you is that you're still carrying the same baggage that led to your previously dysfunctional romantic life. Practicing The Wait involves letting go of the old fears, insecurities, and addictive behaviors that messed you up in the past, and cleaning up your emotional self. That battered old baggage—feelings of being unloved by your parents, fears lingering in the wake of an abusive relationship, body issues, and so on—drives your behavior. That's why unhealthy relationship tends to follow unhealthy relationship, over and over, until the similarities become almost eerie.

Until you can drop that baggage, those patterns aren't likely to change.

FINE-TUNING

When the two of us speak about our relationship and The Wait in front of live audiences or on radio or television, we hear plenty of questions from people of strong faith who are already getting their minds right and syncing up their choices with God's will. They're looking for ideas on how they can be more disciplined, patient, and proactive.

If you've already been practicing The Wait without knowing it, and it's going pretty well, here are some fine-tuning tips that could make it even better.

Check in regularly with your accountability partners. If you can put together a support circle of men or women who are all practicing The Wait, that's gold. Everyone gets the challenges of celibacy and knows what everybody else is going through. But if you can't find others doing The Wait, don't worry. All you really need is a small group of people you're close to who care about your well-being. Meet with them regularly and conduct your meetings based on the following ground rules: total honesty, constructive criticism, and no judgment.

Your accountability partners will pat you on the back when you make great choices and won't let you off the hook when you make choices that undermine The Wait. They'll help you get back on the horse if you weaken and sleep with an ex. They'll cheer you on when you sign up for the master classes you've been talking about taking for two years. They'll keep you honest and on track, even when The Wait seems to be dragging on.

Set clear goals and time frames. True, you don't have control over when God will bring you and your intended spouse together. However, that doesn't mean you don't get some control over timing. Set specific goals for yourself, such as a certain salary or a target weight you want to reach. Lay down equally specific schedules: "I will make executive vice president by the end of 2017." You might not know when your ideal mate is coming, but that doesn't mean you can't exercise some control over the rest of the process.

Celebrate. The Wait shouldn't be a grim trudge through daily obligations. It should be a joyful daily discovery of what you're really capable of. So when you reach a milestone, reward yourself and celebrate your progress! There's absolutely nothing wrong with going out on the town with friends to celebrate a promotion, or treating yourself to a trip to a Caribbean beach as a reward for getting your financial affairs in order. Just be sure that your celebration doesn't undermine the work you're doing: no backsliding into bed with anyone, no matter how attractive. Set up your celebrations well in advance so you have some incentive.

Pray. As we've mentioned, this one should be elementary. God is at the core of The Wait; you're doing all of this to give him room to work in your life. So check in with him even more often than you do with your accountability partners. We suggest a daily prayer specifically about The Wait, asking for strength and discipline and listening to the Lord speak to your spirit. He will reveal wonders to you if you're quiet and learn to recognize His voice.

Keep a journal so you can see how far you've come. One big reason some people fall into complacency and stall is because they lose any sense of what they've accomplished. Journaling is the best way to keep track of where you were and where you are now. It doesn't matter whether you use a Tumblr blog, a video diary, or an old-fashioned leather-bound book and a pen. Journal from the first day of The Wait to the last, capturing as much detail as you can.

When you feel tired or discouraged that you're running in place, go back and read your journal entries. You'll see how far you have come in a surprisingly short time. If your journal is online and public, you might even get encouraging comments from well-wishers cheering you on. That always helps raise the spirits and stiffen the will.

Heal the past. Everyone who waits comes to the dance toting something from their past: rivalries, trauma, anger, you name it. But it's precisely those ugly pieces of luggage that led you to the promiscuity or the multiple failed relationships. If you want to wait, you've got to let the past go and move on. That often means reaching out to people who have hurt you and making peace with them. We know that's difficult, but here's the most effective way to do that: forgive.

For someone practicing The Wait, forgiveness is power. By forgiving others for their treatment of you, you free yourself from anger, regret, or guilt. You take back your power by taking the high ground—God's ground. Have you ever looked at someone from your past and thought, "They don't deserve forgiveness"? Maybe they don't, but remember that it's not about the other person; it's about you. Confronting and forgiving turns the page, closes the book, and lets you heal.

FINAL THOUGHTS

Neither of us was perfect in the way that we waited. We both made mistakes. We both questioned what God was doing and resisted His will. We became discouraged and confused. We're far from perfect. The one thing we did that allowed us to date, fall in love, marry, and come to you with this gift was to put our total faith in God. He threw us some surprises and challenges, but we never wavered in our belief that He was building a foundation under us that would lead us to glory.

The experience of our romance has taught us so much, but this is one of the most surprising things we've learned:

God is romantic.

Admittedly, that's probably not the first word that comes to mind when you think of the Lord. Demanding, sure. Benevolent, absolutely. But romantic? Think about it. What's more romantic than knowing that there is a perfect person (truly, more than one) for you out there in the world and that he or she is slowly walking his or her winding path toward the place and time when you will meet? You don't know when you'll cross paths or how. You don't know if you'll instantly be attracted or just be friends for a while. All you know is that there is a love of your life who will one day be yours when you're ready. At the risk of repeating the film metaphor from *Produced by Faith,* God's directing a really great script.

Wherever you are in your journey to find the love of your life, our best advice is to trust God and have faith. You can trust God to do right by you if you do right by him—entering The Wait honestly, with good intentions, and doing your best to honor your commitment. Just don't give up. And if you fall, don't dwell on it. Dust yourself off. Ask for forgiveness and get right back to your commitment. Sometimes, God doesn't bring people into our lives in the way we expect or in the time we expect, but that doesn't mean he's not working in your life to make wonderful things happen. It just means that you have to have faith.

Great things are coming. Better yet, great things are already here! Even if love isn't on your doorstep at this very moment, with every day that passes, you're becoming wiser, stronger, and more in control of who you're becoming. That's amazing. Believe in God just as He believes in you. Keep your focus, take a deep breath, and don't give up on The Wait. Let God work on you and within you. Right now—today—is the beginning of the relationship, and the life, that you've always dreamed of and the one you've been praying for.

Acknowledgments

We are eternally grateful for all the help we've received to help get our story told. We want to thank God and our Lord and Savior Jesus Christ for the opportunity to share our lives together and to share our story, too. We want to thank Jonathan Merkh and the incredible Howard Books family; our wonderful book agent Jillian Manus; the dynamic publicity duo Julie Solomon and Beth Hood; our friend and super talented coauthor Tim Vandehey; and to our family, friends, and fans—we thank you immensely for your love, prayers, and support. We wouldn't be where we are without any of you.